Mama's Bread

I left my potato in the coals
Because even Tommy laughed at me
For losing at Kick-The-Can,
So I scuffed my way home from the bonfire hungry.

A whiff of wood-burning heat,
Fragrance of hot bread
Billowed through the doorway.

Surprised by any good thing that night,
I watched Mama take a loaf from the oven,
Break open its ruddy brown crust.

Fierce aroma,
Walnuts and hot honey
Breathed through the room
With all the tenderness
Mama had folded into the dough.

Apricot butter
Drenched my handful of bread
And dripped through my fingers,
Which could not hold
All the healing.

Doris Ida Child Black

Written by my mother, who shared these memories and gave me my own.

Master Bread Making Using Whole Wheat

Master Bread Making Using Whole Wheat

By
Diana Ballard

CFI
Springville, Utah

ISBN 13: 978-1-59955-187-6

Published by CFI, an imprint of Cedar Fort, Inc., 2373 W. 700 S., Springville, UT 84663
Distributed by Cedar Fort, Inc., www.cedarfort.com

LIBRARY OF CONGRESS CATALOGING-IN-PUBLICATION DATA

Ballard, Diana.
  Master bread making using whole wheat / Diana Ballard.
     p. cm.
  "A step by step method book."
  Previously published in 1993.
  ISBN 978-1-59955-187-6 (alk. paper)
  1. Bread. 2. Cookery (Wheat) I. Title. II. Title: Whole wheat breadmaking.

  TX769.B19 2008
  641.6'311--dc22

                              2008025467

Cover design by Jen Boss
Cover design © 2009 by Lyle Mortimer
Edited and typeset by Natalie A. Hepworth

Printed in the United States of America
10 9 8 7 6 5 4 3 2 1

Printed on acid-free paper

I'd like to dedicate this book to my mother,
Doris Ida Child Black.

She wrote the poem in the beginning of the book,
which shows how she loved making home a good place to be . . . especially the kitchen.
She taught me by her example how to make good nutritious meals out of very basic food items.
She always had to budget her grocery money carefully,
but somehow managed to feed our large family enough to sustain us.
I hope to show my love and respect for her by sharing ways to make home and hearth a healing place to be.

CONTENTS

ACKNOWLEDGMENTS

There are many people who have contributed to the writing of this book. I owe them all many thanks. My sincere appreciation goes to:

Mr. Tom Dickson of the Blendtec Corporation in Orem, Utah, for his encouragement, ideas, and for the use of his excellent wheat mill and bread mixer as I experimented with many, many recipes.

The Kitchen Resource Company, which allowed me the use of their very efficient Nutrimill, as I researched many electric wheat mills.

The Zojirushi America Corporation, for the use of their bread making machine.

Dr. John Hal Johnson, former professor in the Department of Food Science and Nutrition at Brigham Young University in Provo, Utah, who answered many of my questions about bread making.

Dr. Gur S. Ranhotra, Cereal Chemist and Director of Nutrition Research for the American Institute of Baking in Manhattan, Kansas, who shared valuable research with me.

Maura Bean of the Cereals Group at the USDA Western Regional Laboratory in Berkeley, California, who also answered many questions for on the chemistry of whole wheat bread making.

Mr. Sherman Robinson and his staff at Lehi Roller Mills in Lehi, Utah, who shared valuable information on wheat and whole wheat flour.

Mr. Dick Sperry, formerly of Blendtec Corporation in Orem, Utah who has given much valuable information on bread making chemistry.

Mr. Don Norton, formerly with the English Department of Brigham Young University in Provo, Utah, for his editing and encouragement.

I am most grateful to my husband, Larry, and my family, for their help and patience, as we made many batches of bread, then took the time to write the story of all that bread.

INTRODUCTION

Since the initial publication of this book in 1993, I have heard many success stories from individuals who have acquainted themselves with the principles of whole wheat bread making. Because of this interest and continuing success, I thought it provident to update a few sections of the book while keeping the bread making principles constant. I have also added a section on whole wheat muffins—a fun way to introduce whole wheat into the diets of families and individuals.

My hope is that the reader will enjoy learning to make whole wheat bread, and will also enjoy making memories with loved ones.

Have you ever made a loaf of whole wheat bread and had it turn out as heavy as a brick?

Or have you ever tried to slice your beautiful loaf of homemade wheat bread, only to have each slice crumble into a thousand little pieces?

I, too, have made my share of wheat flour bricks, and I have made plenty of wheat crumble instead of wheat bread.

Many of us have made white bread with some success, yet when we try to make whole wheat bread, we fail miserably. Be consoled that whole wheat flour contains 30 percent more components than white flour. With a little knowledge and practice, we can learn to work with those extra components, and successfully master the art of whole wheat bread making.

The rewards of bread making with whole wheat flour are many. The smell and taste of hot bread in Mother's kitchen is such a sweet remembrance. Don't we all relish the peace, security, and goodness that come from such memories? As you develop your bread-making skills, you'll also be providing these memories for the significant people in your life. If your bread is made with 100 percent whole wheat flour, it is also one of the most nutritious foods known.

One hundred years ago, Thomas Edison stated, "The doctor of the future will give no medicine, but will interest her or his patient in the care of the human frame, in a proper diet, and in the cause and prevention of disease." We now live in that future spoken of by Mr. Edison. Medical scientists are now telling us that a diet based on whole grains, legumes, fruits, and vegetables can help prevent many of the major diseases. Bread that is 100 percent whole wheat has an abundance of nutrients and fiber that are crucial to good health and disease prevention. As an added bonus, wheat bread costs very little to make.

There are many good recipes to choose from when making whole wheat bread. Some recipes call for very basic ingredients (flour, water, yeast, salt, sugar, and oil). Some recipes call for a greater variety of ingredients (all the above, plus honey, molasses, lecithin, dry milk, gluten flour, eggs, dough enhancer, ascorbic acid, and so forth).

The principles of good bread making are constant. If you learn these principles, you can vary the ingredients in the bread and still get excellent results. Experience is by far the best teacher when making bread. Be persistent with your bread-making until you achieve the results you want!

Before You Begin

Before you make your first batch of whole wheat bread, be sure to read through the bread making concepts and instructions at least twice. The first read-through will acquaint you with the principles of whole wheat bread making. The second will solidify the concepts in your mind, making your bread making more successful.

This book is organized into five chapters. The first chapter goes into detail about each ingredient in wheat bread. It also discusses why wheat bread is made the way it is.

The second chapter includes recipes and instructions for basic wheat bread. It includes options for changing the ingredients in the recipes, to create a wide variety of recipes.

The third chapter contains more bread recipes: only enough detail is given to make each recipe.

The fourth chapter will help you solve your bread-making problems.

The fifth chapter is a bonus chapter filled with recipes for making tasty whole wheat muffins, a healthy treat for breakfasts, afternoon snacks, or anytime.

There are kitchen machines that mix and knead bread dough automatically. The dough is then removed to another container, either a bowl or bread pans. I refer to this type machine as a *bread mixer*.

Another type of machine is an automated bread machine that mixes the dough, allows it to rise, then bakes it. Such a machine will only bake one loaf of bread at a time. I refer to one of these machines as a *bread maker*.

When referring to baking temperatures, I always use the Fahrenheit scale. If a recipe bakes at 400 degrees, it is safe to assume that it is 400 degrees Fahrenheit.

CHAPTER 1
Learning the Basics and Nutrients in Wheat

Wheat, also known as the "staff of life," is literally that! More than a third of the world's population receives more than half of their daily caloric needs from wheat. Wheat is the most nutritious of all the grains, being especially rich in vitamin B and proteins.

A wheat kernel is divided into three main parts: the outer layer, called the bran; the inner starchy layer, called the endosperm; and the tiny embryo at the base of the kernel, called the germ.

The outer layer, or the bran, makes up 14 percent of the wheat kernel, and is removed when making white flour. Most of the B vitamins in wheat are contained in the bran layer (although there is still plenty of B complex in the endosperm and germ as well). B vitamins are known to strengthen the nerves. If stress is a part of your life, you can really help yourself by including whole wheat in your diet.

Wheat bran also contains protein, vitamins A, C, and E, biotin, folic acid, inositol, chlorine, calcium, cobalt, choline, copper, iron, fluorine, iodine, magnesium, manganese, phosphorous, potassium, silicon, sodium, sulfur, zinc, and other trace minerals.

Health experts are now telling us that we need more high-fiber foods in our diets. Wheat bran is not only rich in vitamins and minerals, but is also a very good source of dietary fiber. In highly industrialized countries, food is generally more refined than in less developed countries. Interestingly, colon cancer has been one of the highest leading cancer-caused deaths in North America. Yet in Third World countries, where two and one-half times the fiber is consumed, only occasionally does one find a death caused by colon cancer.

High fiber diets have also been linked with low rates of heart disease, constipation, gallstones, diabetes, hemorrhoids, and systemic cancer.

The endosperm of the wheat kernel is the starchy layer. It contains about 83 percent of the wheat protein, and is the source of white flour. All the bran and all the germ have been removed. (Picture courtesy of Lehi Roller Mills)

The protein in wheat flour is low in the amino acid, lysine. In the past, nutrition experts have insisted that wheat must be combined with high lysine foods (corn, beans, milk) in order to have a positive protein balance in the body.

Several studies have been published that shed new light on the benefits of using bread made with wheat flour as a basis for protein in the diet. The studies, which used white bread as the major source of protein, indicate that wheat consumed in sufficient amounts can provide enough lysine to permit a positive protein balance in human adults. This represents a departure from the commonly held belief that wheat alone will not support positive protein balance in non-pregnant, non-lactating human adults.

Those associated with the studies are not suggesting that human adults consume only wheat foods. A mixed diet is always a sensible approach. However, it is good to know that if one was limited to wheat products for their protein needs, for any reason,

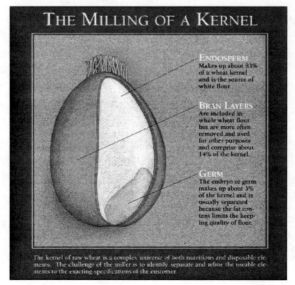

THE MILLING OF A KERNEL

ENDOSPERM
Makes up about 83% of a wheat kernel and is the source of white flour.

BRAN LAYERS
Are included in whole wheat flour but are more often removed and used for other purposes and comprise about 14% of the kernel.

GERM
The embryo or germ makes up about 3% of the kernel and is usually separated because the fat content limits the keeping quality of flour.

The kernel of raw wheat is a complex universe of both nutritious and disposable elements. The challenge of the miller is to identify, separate and refine the useable elements to the exacting specifications of the customer.

even though variety might be compromised, at least the protein requirements could be met.[1]

Wheat germ is the life of the wheat kernel. Although it represents only 3 percent of the kernel, it contains all the nutrients needed to start new wheat growth. Wheat germ is rich in B vitamins, iron, potassium, magnesium, zinc, and protein. Wheat germ also contains wheat germ oil, which is a natural source of Vitamin E. However, because of the oil in the wheat germ, flour millers remove the germ to extend the shelf life of flour.

Whole wheat flour purchased from a miller (with the germ removed) is not much different from whole wheat flour milled at home. This is because the Vitamin E in the germ is destroyed when bread is baked. It is easy to see the reason that millers remove the wheat germ from whole wheat flour or white flour. You do lose a few other nutrients that are in the wheat germ, but many of those nutrients are still available in the bran and endosperm. Wheat germ is simply the very tiny beginning of a miraculous wheat kernel. Therein lies its importance.

Wheat flour is one of the least expensive sources of high quality protein. When compared with animal protein, it is only about one-fourth the cost.

EQUIPMENT AND KITCHEN TOOLS

Following is a list of basic kitchen tools that will help ensure your success:

- liquid measuring cups
- dry ingredient measuring cups
- measuring spoons
- spatula
- large bowl for mixing and/or rising
- small bowl for softening yeast (if you use regular, non-instant yeast)
- bread thermometer for correct water temperature
- rubber scraper to clean dough from bowl
- kitchen scale (if desired) to weigh dough
- small ruler to measure rising dough
- rolling pin (if desired) to form loaves
- pastry brushes to brush shortening on pans, or to brush tops of loaves with milk or butter
- thin cloths to dampen and cover rising loaves
- muffin tins, baking sheets, 8- or 9- inch round or square pans for baking fancy rolls and breads
- cooling racks
- spray-on cooking oil for bread pans
- bread pans

The ideal size pan for whole wheat bread making is a standard size pan (7½ x 3½ x 2¾ inches). If the narrow measurement of the pan is wider than 3 ½ inches, many times the top center of the loaf cannot sustain itself. After baking and cooling, the top center of the loaf will drop down instead of staying well formed and rounded.

There are many different types of construction materials with bread pans. There are aluminum, silicone, glass (Pyrex), and stainless steel. If you have a gas or electric convection oven, or a conventional gas oven, any of these pans should perform well—as long as the size is standard.

If your oven is an electric oven, and is not a convection oven, there is more to consider when choosing pans. Most electric ovens are notorious for uneven heating. Most of the time, the center of the oven is the hottest, with the outside edges being cooler. Periodically, one will have an oven that is just the opposite, with the highest heat around the outside edge. So if someone is baking several loaves of bread at one time, how does one avoid oddly shaped loaves coming out of the oven, due to the uneven heating?

There is one type of pan that seems to overcome the challenge of uneven oven heat. This pan is one made of cast iron. Aluminum, glass, silicone, and stainless steel pans are much lighter, and therefore more convenient than cast iron. Additionally, cast iron pans have generally fallen out of favor with consumers because of their weight, so it can be a small problem to find good cast iron bread pans. Given these challenges, however, the best pans for even heating and temperature maintenance are still, cast iron loaf pans. If an oven has uneven heat distribution, the cast iron pans can help overcome this problem to a large degree. The bread bakes evenly, and develops a golden brown crust.

Several years ago, I found some Lodge cast iron bread pans that were the ideal standard size. I purchased several of them, and recommended them to others. Since that time, Lodge has chosen to discontinue making those loaf pans.

The only manufacturer that I have found is Camp Chef. Camp Chef makes a cast iron loaf pan that is 9 inches long on the inside, tapering to 8½ inches at the bottom. It is 5 inches wide on the inside, tapering down to 4 inches. So, it is a little larger than a standard size loaf pan, but the cast iron construction allows the bread to bake more evenly than any of the standard size pans made of other materials. It will hold 2 pounds of whole wheat bread dough, whereas the standard size pans hold 1¾ pounds of dough (1 lb. 12 oz.).

Even though whole wheat bread dough may stay better formed in standard size pans, it generally bakes better in cast iron pans, even if the pan is a little larger than standard. The bread pan on far left is Camp Chef (wider), the bread pan on far right is Lodge (more narrow). Camp Chef is located at 675 North 600 West, Logan, Utah 84321. They can be reached at 1-800-650-2433 or online at www.campchef.com. These pans can also be found in various sporting goods stores.

Another option is to use a Clay Oven Bread Baker. These clay oven bakers simulate a brick oven, and leave the bread crust chewy and flavorful. They are a little more expensive than cast iron, but make wonderful bread. They, too, may be a little wider than a standard bread pan. Because of the construction material (clay), the bread is so similar to brick oven bread that it may be worth your investment. They are available online.

Another idea that can be interesting and fun to use is a 6-inch round cast iron skillet in the oven. It makes a delightful loaf of round bread. Actually, any cast iron pan can be used to bake bread—the dough will just conform to whatever shape the pan is.

Be willing to experiment a little with bread pans, and become familiar with how your oven heats. It could make a big difference in your finished loaves.

ELECTRIC MILLS

Because wheat contains so much life-giving nutrition, you may want to consider purchasing your own wheat mill. By milling flour at home, you capture 100 percent of the nutrients in the wheat. I'd like to share with you the experience I had in my search for a good wheat mill. It may help you as you decide which mill to purchase.

In 1978, I decided to purchase a wheat mill. Until

that time, I had been using a little hand grinder, which left my wheat flour quite coarse. For years, I heard that stone-ground flour was the best wheat flour available. I was delighted to finally find an electric "stone" mill, and I was convinced it was the ultimate milling machine. So I purchased it, took it home, and used it. However, it milled the flour quite hot and was very slow.

I learned a few years later that the stones (hard sandstones) for the original stone grinding mills were quarried especially for their hardness and porosity. However, because none of these stones were available for in-home use, the stones in my mill (and most other stone mills for home use) were made of aluminum oxide, or silicon carbide. I knew that the stones were gradually wearing out, but when I realized that they were wearing out into my flour, I began looking for another mill.

Then I found a new mill that used two stainless steel grinding surfaces to mill the wheat. I was very pleased with the mill, because I no longer had to worry that my family would be eating residue from aluminum or silicon stones. Because it had stainless steel grinding surfaces, it was also very effective in milling moist or oily grains (rice, peanuts, corn, etc.) Unfortunately, the milling process was hot (165 degrees) like the stone mill. The heat from milling was damaging the gluten in my flour (gluten is the elastic framework that develops during the kneading process, holding the bread together). My bread was always crumbly. The mill was also so slow that I would have to take one afternoon to mill my wheat, and then save the flour until another day to make bread.

Soon after, I was introduced to a micronizing mill that shattered the wheat kernels against steel teeth, instead of rubbing or grinding them between stones or plates. The resulting flour was fine, and also cool enough that the gluten was not damaged (below 135 degrees). The mill was also very fast. I now use this type of mill and have been very pleased with it.

The Nutrimill is a very fast, cool, and quiet micronizing mill. It mills wheat and other dry grains into fine flour, making it very convenient to mill flour at home. (Picture courtesy of Kitchen Resource Company). Blendtec Corporation, the first to manufacture an electric micronizing mill, also makes a very good wheat mill. It mills wheat with very little damage to the resulting flour. This milling process alone can make a large difference in your whole wheat bread. (Picture courtesy of Blendtec Corporation.)

These two grain mills are excellent mills that are reasonably priced and available online (just type the name of the mill into a search engine such as Google to find the nearest retailer). You can also check for wheat mills in kitchen gourmet shops, specialty food outlets, grain outlets, or country living catalogs. If you purchase a type of mill other than a micronizing mill, make certain that it mills wheat into fine flour without getting much above 135 degrees. Also, make certain that your mill does not have stones that are wearing out into your flour.

HAND MILLS

Hand wheat mills take longer to use than electric mills, but do not require electricity. They are slower than electric mills and wear out more rapidly. Even so, a hand mill is especially good to have on hand in the event of a power failure.

Hand milled flour needs to be very fine if it is going to be used for bread. If you do purchase a hand mill for yourself, make sure that it mills flour very fine. If it has stones, make sure that the stones are not made with any type of aluminum or materials that could wear out into your flour.

There are several good hand mills available. Pictured is a Country Living Grain Mill, available online at www.countrylivinggrainmill.com.

There is also a grain crusher/roller mill made in Italy

by OMC Marcato. It is called the Marga, and is available online through many different retailers. It is an excellent multipurpose hand mill.

There is also a Family Grain Mill made in Germany by Messerschmidt. It has been around for about thirty-five years, and has proven itself to be well made and efficient. Retailers can be found online, or Blendtec and Bosch carry the Marga in their outlets.

BREAD MIXERS

I believe that everyone should learn to make whole wheat bread by hand before purchasing a bread mixer. The experience is invaluable. However, whether you have made bread by hand, a bread mixer is a great tool to have in the kitchen.

Once you've decided to go look for a bread mixer, there are a few tips that may help you in making your choice.

1. Make certain that the machine is made with as many safety features as possible.
2. Make sure, as with the wheat mill, that the noise level is tolerable for you. Because wheat bread dough is so heavy, look for a bread mixer that has at least 700 watts of power. Anything less may not adequately knead your dough.
3. Make certain that the machine has been made well and will last a long time—check the warranty.
4. Make sure that the machine has the proper capacity for your needs. If you need four loaves each time you make bread, don't settle for a machine that makes only two loaves.

If the bread machine has other functions (food processing, blending, etc.) make certain that the parts are easy to assemble, use, take apart, and clean. Otherwise, the machine may end up gathering dust.

The Blendtec Corporation manufactures a bread mixer that is built specifically to make excellent bread. The kneading arms have a unique configuration that maximizes the gluten development in bread dough. It has plenty of power and is also very versatile as a kitchen machine. (Picture courtesy of Blendtec Corporation.) Bosch also makes a bread mixer that is reliable and quiet during operation. It is built to handle large amounts of dough and is versatile in the kitchen.

Both of these machines are priced reasonably and deserve consideration. Most importantly, when looking for a wheat mill or bread mixer, take enough time to find exactly what you want. These could become the most frequently used appliances in your kitchen.

AUTOMATIC BREAD MAKERS

An automatic bread maker that makes really good whole wheat bread is great to have in any household. Your whole wheat bread, however, will only be as good as the machine that makes it.

When considering an automatic bread maker, be aware of several features that are especially good for whole wheat bread making. One important feature is a kneading arm that kneads first one direction, then the other. The gluten strands develop better with two-directional kneading.

Another feature that is helpful is a programmable cycle, where you can program how long you want each cycle to last. Or, the machine may have a separate wheat bread cycle. For example, whole wheat dough takes longer to knead and raise than white bread dough. It is nice to have a bread maker that can be programmed, or has its own whole wheat bread cycle.

My personal choice in an automatic bread maker is the Zojirushi for several

reasons. It has dual kneading arms that reverse directions during kneading, and it has a programmable cycle that works well for wheat bread. (Picture courtesy of Zojirushi Corporation.) Panasonic also makes a good bread maker that is very reliable. I have found that these two machines are a little more costly than some of the others in the market. My experience has shown me, however, that the success of my wheat bread is directly related to the quality of my bread maker.

BUYING WHEAT

If you choose to buy wheat and mill it yourself, make sure that the wheat you purchase is either hard white spring wheat, or hard red winter or spring wheat. All types of wheat are high in fiber, and may cause digestive difficulty until you are accustomed to using wheat in your diet. If you are able to eat whole wheat products with no difficulty, it probably will not matter whether you use hard red or hard white wheat.

The wheat you purchase should be high in protein (13 percent or more).

There are six different proteins in wheat, but only two of these proteins will develop into gluten. These two proteins (called gliadin and glutenin) need to make up an adequate percentage of the proteins in the wheat. Otherwise, your bread will not develop gluten. There are types of soft wheat available, (producing what is called whole-wheat pastry flour), but they are lower in protein (6–10 percent) and do not make good bread. These flours, however, are great for cakes and cookies.

A high percentage of bread making protein in wheat does not guarantee that the wheat will make good bread. It is just the foundation of good bread making. There are other factors to consider as well. A farmer may plant the same variety of wheat from year to year, but that doesn't ensure that the miller or baker will get a uniform product.

Variances in the performance of whole wheat are caused by many factors, some of which are moisture content, gluten strength, mixing tolerance, and ash and starch composition. So, when you purchase wheat with a certain percentage of protein and find success with it, be aware that if you purchase wheat again with the same protein—either the same kind, or a different kind—the performance may be different.

For example, I have hard white spring wheat that is 15 percent protein. The bread making proteins are adequate, but the bread I make with this wheat is not as acceptable as bread that I make using a hard red winter wheat that is only 13 percent protein. It is because of variances in some of those other factors named above. Even in large bakeries, the baker has to make adjustments to his recipe on an ongoing basis. Temperature, humidity, moisture content, and many other factors contribute to the degree of success. So you can see that whole wheat bread making can be a bit complex. Hopefully, as you find the right wheat or wheat flour, it will become the foundation for further success.

As was mentioned earlier, hard white wheat and hard red wheat make equally good bread. They are also equally nutritious. White wheat has a milder flavor, and red wheat a heartier flavor. Many times, distributors charge more money for white wheat, but the nutritional and bread making characteristics are the same as red wheat. It just depends upon growing conditions, and all those factors that were just discussed above.

Following are a few sources for good bread making wheat. Most of these dealers will ship their products. It is wise to purchase wheat in small quantities, and then make bread with it. Then you will know whether or not to buy it in bulk. If you purchase enough wheat to last a while, you won't have to continually experiment as the commercial bakeries do. You'll come to trust your method because your wheat performance will be consistent.

You can also check with your local health food stores, or kitchen specialty shops.

- Arrowhead Mills, The Hain Celestial Group, 4600 Sleepytime Drive, Boulder, Colorado 80301 www.arrowheadmills.com
- Lehi Roller Mills, 833 East Main Street, Lehi, Utah 84043, 1-877-311-3566
- Wheat Montana Farms, 10778 Highway 287, Three Forks, Montana, 59752 1-800-535-2798 www.wheatmontana.com
- Heartland Mill Incorporated, Route 1 Box 2, Marienthal, Kansas 67863, 1-800-232-8533. www.heartlandmill.com
- Honeyville Grain Inc., 3570 West 7200 North Honeyville, Utah 84314, 1-435-279-8197 www.honeyvillegrain.com

MILLING WHEAT

After purchasing your wheat, you will want to mill it and make bread with it. Wheat needs to be milled fine enough to allow the gluten framework to develop during the kneading process. If the wheat is too coarsely ground, the gluten cannot be developed. Most electric wheat mills for home use are designed so that the finest mill setting is used to make very fine pastry flour. Bread making flour does not need to be quite that fine, so use the next setting for bread flour.

If you are using a hand mill for your wheat, you should mill the flour on the finest setting. Depending on your mill, you may have to mill the flour a second time to get it fine enough for bread. You will know that your flour is too coarse for bread making if it is the texture of uncooked germade, or Cream of Wheat™. You may want to buy a small amount of whole wheat flour at the grocery store, and compare it with your home milled flour, just to make sure you have the right texture setting on your mill.

If your mill gets hot (135 degrees or higher) when it has to grind fine, the gluten may be damaged from the high milling temperature. If your flour seems hot after it is milled, use your kitchen thermometer to check the temperature of the flour. You may choose to leave your flour a little on the coarse side in order to keep your milling temperature down around 135 degrees.

When milling wheat into flour, one cup of grain yields almost one and one-half cups of flour. For example, if your recipe calls for three cups of flour, mill only about two and a fourth cups of wheat.

Storing Wheat

You may decide to purchase hard wheat in bulk so that you have plenty on hand for bread making. If you do, make certain that the moisture content of your wheat is no higher than 10 percent.

Make certain that your wheat is very clean. Wheat generally will not be troubled by weevil if it is thoroughly cleaned before marketing. Compare the wheat from several outlets before you purchase it in bulk. Not only will you avoid having weevil in your wheat, but also small rocks or other foreign matter that can damage your wheat mill.

Wheat is generally sold in large paper transport bags. After purchasing your wheat, it is best to repackage it either in metal cans, plastic buckets with rubber seals in the lids, or glass containers. The repackaging will keep out insects and vermin. If humidity is a problem in your location, it is a good idea to locate a cannery that will help you can your wheat for storage in sealed metal cans. If desired, small-scale canning equipment can be purchased or rented for home use.

Wheat will keep indefinitely, with nutrients intact, if stored properly. Keep wheat away from insects, moisture, and excessive heat.

Several old wives' tales circulate about wheat storage. One of them is that bay or mint leaves will keep weevil out. As was mentioned earlier, clean wheat is the best deterrent to weevil. However, insects may be killed by freezing wheat for 7–14 days at 0 degrees. There are two schools of thought on the use of dry ice to kill weevil or to seal cans of wheat. One belief is that an atmosphere of carbon dioxide will destroy weevil—and this has proven to be true. About one-fourth pound of dry ice is placed on top of two gallons of wheat in a bucket. The remainder of the bucket is filled with wheat and the lid is loosely placed on the bucket for six hours. It is then sealed tightly so that there is an oxygen-deprived atmosphere inside the bucket for seven to ten days. This kills any weevil and eggs.

The other school of thought is that although dry ice

provides an oxygen-deprived environment, it also introduces moisture into its environment as it evaporates. In a warm, humid climate, this can definitely shorten the storage life of your wheat. It may be that wheat in warm, damp climates is best stored in sealed cans.

If you want to eliminate the chance of having any weevil in your wheat, you can put it in a freezer at 0 degrees for two weeks. This kills any weevil and their eggs. This works for flour as well. If weevil does get in your wheat or flour, simply use a screen to clean it. If the infestation is heavy you may choose to replace the wheat or flour with new product.

Basic Bread Ingredients

WHOLE WHEAT FLOUR

The most basic ingredient in wheat bread is 100 percent whole wheat flour, milled from high protein, low moisture wheat. If you do not mill your own flour, you can purchase whole wheat flour from a reputable miller. If you purchase flour from a miller, or grocer, the wheat germ will have been removed. The germ contains oil that causes the flour to start going rancid after three or four weeks at room temperature. Lehi Roller Mills sells very high quality wheat

flour (it is especially formulated for good bread making). Gold Medal Flour will sometimes have good wheat flour as well; one just has to buy it and try it.

Most wheat mill dealers who want to sell their mills will tell potential customers that wheat flour needs to be used immediately after milling in order to get all the nutrients before they oxidize. This tactic is usually effective in helping sell mills. The actual truth of the matter is that wheat flour may be stored for several weeks at room temperature without losing substantial nutrition.

There is evidence that the baking process actually destroys more nutrients than those lost in leaving wheat flour out at room temperature for a few days or even weeks. Technical data indicates that the chemical makeup of freshly-milled wheat flour and its digestibility in the human body is of greater concern nutritionally than the amount of time that lapses between the time the wheat is milled and its use in baking.[2] According to calculations done with current statistics, the actual nutrient loss in wheat flour during the baking process is very minimal as well.[3]

If desired, you may store wheat flour in the refrigerator or freezer; this will slow down the oxidation of the wheat germ. Remember to let the flour sit out and come to room temperature before using it to make bread.

Whole wheat flour contains not only the endosperm of the wheat kernel, but a small amount of wheat germ and a large amount of wheat bran. The germ and the bran are the components that cause so much difficulty in bread making with 100 percent whole wheat flour. Let's talk for a moment about wheat bran and wheat germ.

As was mentioned earlier, wheat bran is very nutritious and is rich in dietary fiber. However, after milling, wheat bran has rough, sharp edges that can damage the gluten framework of whole wheat dough as it is being kneaded and also as it rises. With bran present in bread dough, the gluten takes longer to develop than if it were absent (8–10 minutes of kneading wheat bread as opposed to 3–5 minutes of kneading white bread). For these reasons, I never add extra bran to my whole wheat bread dough. It already has sufficient with the whole wheat flour in the recipe.

The oil that naturally occurs in wheat germ is valuable in whole wheat bread, but much of the vitamin E in the germ bakes out during the baking process. Wheat germ also contains an agent called glutathione that breaks down gluten in whole wheat bread dough. The longer the germ is

in contact with the gluten that has developed in the dough, the more damage it can do to the dough. For this reason, I never add extra wheat germ to my wheat bread. As you read, you will learn other steps you can take to minimize the damage from the glutathione. We will discuss them further as the bread making process unfolds.

Substituting White and Other Flours

If you choose to substitute white flour for any of the wheat flour in your bread, there are some tips to remember. White flour purchased for use in bread making, should be labeled "Better for Bread," as opposed to "All-Purpose." All-purpose flour does not contain the strong gluten-making proteins that are contained in bread making flour. Instead, it is used for making quick breads, cookies, cakes, and pie crusts. You don't want or need strong gluten strands in these types of baked goods.

Bleached white flour is derived from the endosperm layer of the wheat kernel. When commercial mills process wheat into white flour, the bran and the germ are removed (along with all of their nutrients). The remaining endosperm layer is bleached white (or left in its natural off-white color for unbleached flour). Of the sixteen nutrients that are removed from wheat flour when it is processed, only three major nutrients are reintroduced into the white flour (thiamin, riboflavin, and niacin). The addition of these nutrients has helped eradicate vitamin deficiency diseases such as pellagra. With the exception of these three nutrients, wheat flour contains more nutrients and fiber than processed white flour.[4]

Unbleached flour is not any more nutritious than bleached flour, although some people prefer using it because it hasn't undergone the bleaching process. Both bleached and unbleached flour are classified as white flour, although bleached flour is a little whiter in color. There are two big reasons why white flour is used both privately and commercially for bread making, even though it is nutritionally inferior to wheat flour.

During the mid 1600s, white bread became the bread of royalty because of its light, delicate color and flavor. Consequently, common people began to wish for this luxury food, thereby creating a demand for white bread. White bread has been with us ever since that time.

The second reason that white flour is used in bread making is that it is easier to get good results than with whole wheat flour. If you have ever made white bread, you know how easy it is to knead white bread dough and how little time it takes to develop the gluten (3–5 minutes by hand). With the bran and germ removed, there is nothing to impede the development of the proteins into long strands of gluten.

If you choose to use white flour in your bread making, you may run across white flour in a grocery store that is on sale for a great price, although the brand of flour may be unfamiliar to you. Many less expensive brands of flour are inconsistent in the amount of bread making proteins that are present. Many batches of bread made with white flour fail because the bread is made with low quality flour. If you have ever had this experience, you know how frustrating it can be. Gold Medal Bread Making Flour is usually a little higher in price than other brands, but it makes consistently good white bread.

Lehi Roller Mills in Lehi, Utah, also sells consistently good-quality bread making flour. You can check other mills for high quality white flour, or you can purchase high quality bread making flour in your grocery store. There truly can be a large difference in the quality of the different brands of white flour, and their success in bread making.

Up to one-third of the whole wheat flour in any

bread recipe can be interchanged with either bleached or unbleached white flour.

If you want to substitute cracked wheat for some of your wheat flour, substitute it for no more than one-eighth of your wheat flour. Be sure to cook the cracked wheat or soak it overnight to soften it.

Barley, rice, millet, oat, bean, and corn flour may be substituted for one-third of the wheat flour in any bread recipe. Each of these flours manifests unique characteristics. Consequently, the texture of your bread will be different from that of 100 percent whole wheat bread.

Rice and bean flours tend to be heavy, so use one-fourth or less of each of these ingredients.

Freshly ground rye flour may be used in place of no more than one-fourth of your wheat flour. It is wise to use gluten flour when using rye flour in your bread.

Yeast

Yeast is a living plant that needs warmth and moisture to grow. Warm bread dough provides a perfect place for yeast growth, but yeast still needs food in a form that it can use. Yeast thrives best on sugar, so when yeast comes in contact with the flour in bread dough, enzymes in yeast convert the starch in flour into a sugar.

Flour does not provide all the food yeast needs, so other yeast food is usually added to bread dough (sugar, honey, or molasses). Yeast then ferments these sugars into alcohol and carbon dioxide gas. The gas is trapped in the gluten network, causing bread dough to rise. The process continues until the oxygen in the dough is used up. This fermentation process is desirable in the dough, for it gives bread a good flavor. However, if dough is left to rise too long, the yeast quits working, and the alcohol in the dough increases. This rising level of alcohol can kill the yeast. It also damages the gluten.

The resulting loaf of bread will be compact, heavy, and will have a strong smell of alcohol. For this reason, watch your dough closely. If necessary, measure it as it rises to ensure that it does not rise more than double its original size.

There are three basic types of yeast. The most powerful yeast with the greatest rising ability is compressed yeast. It is more perishable than dry yeast because the yeast cells are live and active, and must be used within six weeks. Because the yeast cells are alive and active, it may be added directly to bread dough. It is not as readily available as the other two types.

The second type of yeast, and also the next most powerful is instant, rapid-rise yeast (SAF, Fermipan, Fleischmann's Rapid Rise Yeast). This yeast contains cells that are alive but not active. The outer shell on each dry yeast granule is soft enough that it does not need to be pre-softened in warm water before being added to other bread ingredients. It will absorb liquid as it is mixed directly into the dough. It can be added to bread dough after the first one or two cups of flour are added.

The least powerful yeast for whole wheat bread making is regular active dry yeast (Fleischmann's, Red Star). The yeast cells are alive, but are not active. The outer shell on each yeast granule is very hard and needs to be softened in warm water (85–110 degrees) for five to ten minutes before being added to other bread ingredients. Because it is less powerful than instant or compressed yeast, it takes 20–25 percent more of this yeast than the other two types to get the same results.

You may want to add a half teaspoon sugar or molasses to the dissolving water; it gives yeast a little food to begin growing. If your yeast does not grow after five minutes, it may be old. In that case, you will need fresh yeast.

You will recall that wheat germ contains an agent called glutathione, which breaks down the gluten in whole wheat bread dough. Interestingly, this agent is also present in yeast.

Glutathione in the yeast will not affect the quality of your bread as long as it stays in the yeast cell. Only under adverse conditions will the glutathione leak out. Compressed yeast retains the strength of its yeast cells very effectively, and generally has little to no problems. Instant yeast does not need to be dissolved in water, so it is less likely to release unwanted glutathione.

To avoid any glutathione release, make sure that the dough or flour temperature is 75 degrees or higher when adding instant yeast.[5] However, if you are using active dry yeast, you need to be very careful that your dissolving water is no cooler than 100 degrees. Glutathione will leak out of the yeast cells very rapidly in cool water, causing your dough strength to be weakened. For this reason, I prefer using instant yeast. Not only is it more readily available than compressed yeast, but it is more powerful than active dry yeast, and has less of a problem with glutathione release.

The recipes in this book will call for instant yeast. If your freshly milled flour is very warm (over 120 degrees), make sure the liquid in your bread recipe is a little cooler than 90 degrees. Otherwise, the heat from the liquid, the heat from the flour, and the heat generated from kneading may overheat the dough and kill the yeast.

PURCHASING AND STORING YEAST

Use only fresh yeast in your bread making; old yeast just does not perform well. If you purchase compressed yeast, store it in the refrigerator, but do not allow it to freeze. Freezing temperatures will kill the live yeast cells. Both instant, fast-rise yeast, and active dry yeast are sold in large quantity packages. The best place to store either type is unopened in a freezer at 0–10 degrees. A lower temperature could kill the yeast; a higher temperature will shorten its shelf life.

Once a package is opened, exposure to air, moisture, and warmth causes yeast to deteriorate. So, pour the yeast into a Ziploc™ freezer bag, expel the excess air, seal the bag, and store it in the freezer. It should keep for 3–6 months. The freezer slows down the loss of potency. Each time bread is made, use the yeast right out of the freezer bag, adding it to the bread ingredients (or dissolve in warm water if it is active dry). Expel the excess air, re-seal it, and return it to the freezer.

SOURDOUGH AND YEAST-FREE BREADS

If you have no yeast on hand, and want or need to make bread, wild yeast (or sourdough starter) may be used. Wild yeast grows from spores in the air. Some yeast spores respond very well in bread while others do not. For this reason, whole wheat bread making with wild yeast is always an adventure. If you desire to try it, refer to a good sourdough cookbook for instructions.

I've been asked about making yeast-free bread. Some home bakers try to make yeast bread without yeast, and then allow the bread to sit for one or two days to rise naturally. Yeast spores from the air land on the bread dough, causing fermentation to occur, and natural yeast is created. The only problem is that not all yeast spores make bread rise. You may end up with 90 percent of yeast spores that do nothing for the texture and height of your dough. Wheat bread dough also creates its own yeast. So, technically, the bread is still not yeast free.

If you want bread that is really yeast free, it is probably best to find a good yeast-free cookbook for recipes that use baking powder or baking soda for leavening.

LIQUID

Water, milk, potato water, or buttermilk will fill the requirement for liquid in whole wheat bread.

Water allows the flavor of the wheat to be more pronounced and is the least expensive of the liquid options.

Milk (including reconstituted powdered milk) causes the bread to toast more evenly and quickly. Milk can also cause the bread to rise higher and have a finer texture than water. Breads stay fresher longer when made with milk. However, any milk except evaporated milk needs to be scalded and cooled before use. Scalding the milk kills the enzymes that adversely soften bread dough.

Potato water gives greater volume, as does milk, but gives bread a coarse texture.

Buttermilk causes the dough to be more tender, and adds a distinctive flavor to wheat bread. If you choose to use buttermilk in your bread, use buttermilk for half the liquid requirement, and water or scalded milk for the rest. Too much buttermilk can make bread dough so tender that it falls apart. Also, make sure that you scald the buttermilk before using it. The culture can interfere with the yeast.

Yogurt can be substituted for one-fourth of the water or milk in a bread recipe. It gives a strong yogurt flavor to wheat bread. It must be scalded and cooled before using.

Tomato juice makes a flavorful loaf of bread when used as the liquid. It is best when used with a single-loaf bread maker. It can be used instead of the water in any recipe.

OIL AND FAT

Oil or fat is used in bread to increase elasticity. It also produces a more tender crumb. By including oil or fat in your bread, the volume increases, the bread browns more evenly, and it stays fresh longer.

Because oil tenderizes dough, never use too much oil or fat in your bread. It will shorten the gluten strands in the bread, making it crumbly, with less volume. It will be more like cake (this may sound good, but have you ever tried to make a sandwich out of cake slices?). One tablespoon of vegetable oil for every four cups of flour is sufficient.

By using one tablespoon of oil or fat for every four cups of flour, your bread will contain 12 percent fat (5 percent of that fat occurs naturally in the wheat germ, leaving only 7 percent from the added oil). If bread needs a little fat or oil as one of the ingredients, use only what is necessary.

There are two factors to consider when deciding which oil or fat to use in your bread. One factor is nutrition.

Which oil or fat will be the healthiest? The other factor is success in bread making. Which oil or fat will produce the best result in the bread?

Nutritionally speaking, the healthiest oil to use is lecithin, which is derived from soybeans. Not only is lecithin rich in nutrients, but it is known to help emulsify extra cholesterol in the body. Vegetable oils (such as corn, sunflower, or sesame) are also healthy to use in bread making. Vegetable oil, in small amounts, may actually be beneficial to the heart and arteries.

Butter may be used to fill the fat requirement. Some health experts believe, however, that because butter is high in cholesterol, and is a saturated fat, it should be used very sparingly, if at all. Others claim that because it is a natural product, without being chemically altered, the body is able to assimilate it with no ill effect. You will have to choose whether or not to use butter in your bread making. Some of the recipes in the automatic bread maker section call for butter. If desired, you may substitute lecithin or vegetable oil (use ⅓ more oil than butter; use only ½ the amount of lecithin).

The least nutritious of the fats are lard and shortening. Lard is basically animal fat. Shortening is usually made from vegetable oil that has had hydrogen introduced into it to make it solid. The hydrogenation process creates a product that, like lard, is linked to serious heart disease and various cancers. If you choose to use either of these two types of fat, do so sparingly.

The other factor to consider when choosing your oil or fat is product success. I prefer using lecithin in my bread—not only for its nutritional benefits, but for the binding and emulsifying effect it has on bread dough. It improves moisture tolerance and uniform suspension of ingredients. It also acts as an antioxidant, stabilizing fats and oils, reducing rancidity, and prolonging freshness.

However, a different type of vegetable oil or fat is needed in addition to produce a more tender crumb. As a binder, 1 ½ teaspoons of liquid or granular lecithin per loaf is sufficient. Most whole wheat bread only needs an additional 1 ½ tablespoons of other oil for the texture. Granulated lecithin is available in most health food stores for convenient measuring. For greater ease when using liquid lecithin, measure it into the additional vegetable oil, and then add both to the recipe together.

At times, I want my bread to be exceptionally tender (for gift giving, or for special occasions). When this is the case, I choose to use butter that is at room temperature. I use one-third less butter than oil, because oil absorbs into flour at a higher rate than butter. Butter, if mixed into dough while soft, but still in a solid state, coats the gluten without totally absorbing into the flour. It helps the dough to rise more easily, and creates a more tender loaf during the baking process.

Whether you use oil or fat, make sure it is fresh. Rancid oil or fat should never be used in bread making.

Bread can be made without any oil or fat, as in the case of sourdough bread. The dough will be a little less elastic, and the finished loaves will have a dry, coarse texture.

There is one other way that fats are used in bread making. Shortening has been used for years to grease pans, and oil has been used to lubricate the surface of bread dough as it rises. I prefer using spray-on cooking oil. There are several brands available in grocery stores, PAM™ being the most common. It is easier to use than shortening, contains fewer fat grams than shortening, and is made with lecithin, which is very nutritious. For this reason, my bread pans and bread bowls are sprayed rather than greased or oiled.

Salt

Salt brings out the flavor of the other ingredients in the bread. It also controls the fermentation process. If you have ever made bread and left out the salt, you may have encountered bread that rose too high and then collapsed on itself. Not only was the bread tasteless, but flat as well. If salt needs to be deleted for health reasons, be sure to watch the dough carefully that it doesn't rise too high at any stage.

Salt should never be added to the liquid in which the yeast is dissolving, because it may inhibit or kill the yeast.

Sugar

Sugar feeds the yeast and adds flavor to the bread. Too little sugar can prevent oven browning, while too much sugar causes excess oven browning. This is helpful to know whenever you choose to alter any recipe. White sugar, brown sugar, honey, or molasses may be used, although molasses is an especially good food for yeast. Dairy whey can also provide food for the yeast. However, dairy whey is rich in minerals and salts; it can cause inconsistent effects on the dough. Be judicious with its use.

Whole wheat bread can be made without a sweetening

agent, but the yeast will take longer to work. It has to convert the starch in the flour into sugar before it can be used to feed the yeast. 1 tablespoon of sugar or honey per loaf is sufficient to feed the yeast.

When Optional Ingredients are Needed

The only additional ingredient that may be necessary to the success of your bread is vital wheat gluten. However, it is listed as an optional ingredient because it is not always needed. As you read through the section describing gluten flour and its use in whole wheat bread, you will know just when it is needed.

The other ingredients listed here are truly optional. If you correctly apply the basic principles of whole wheat bread making, your bread should turn out very well. The use of optional ingredients will just enhance something that is already good.

If you experience poor results without the use of optional ingredients, it is most often old yeast, or poor bread making wheat to begin with. If new yeast can be used, the optional ingredients (including gluten flour) may help make up for poor bread making wheat.

Vital Wheat Gluten

Vital wheat gluten (called *gluten flour* throughout this book) is extracted from high protein wheat. The wheat is milled, and the bran and germ are removed. The starch is then washed away, leaving the gluten. It is dried and milled into flour. When added to bread dough, it acts as a binder to make dough more elastic and keep bread from crumbling.

Do not confuse vital wheat gluten with high gluten flour. They are two completely different products.

There are several instances when you may need gluten flour:

- If your wheat is too coarse, the gluten that naturally occurs in the wheat flour will not develop properly during kneading. Flour can be softened by soaking it in water overnight, but the gluten will not develop any better. In this case, gluten flour will help bind the bread together and prevent crumbling.
- The process of kneading develops gluten. If you are unable to knead your bread long enough to develop the gluten, your bread will have large cells and will crumble very easily after baking. Sometimes, automatic bread makers don't knead

the wheat bread dough long enough to completely develop the gluten. In either of these cases, gluten flour will help bind the bread together so that it does not fall apart when it is sliced.

- After wheat is milled into flour, the bran may have sharp, jagged edges that can damage the gluten in your dough. Adding extra gluten flour may help compensate for this damage.

- If your bread consistently turns out crumbly, it may be that your wheat does not have all the components in the necessary proportions to make good bread. In this case, as in the others listed above, add 3–4 tablespoons of gluten flour per loaf of bread to your dough. That should solve any of these difficulties. If the gluten flour makes little to no difference, there may be other factors to consider. The end of chapter 4 contains troubleshooting help.

Too much gluten flour in a recipe can make the bread tough and rubbery, so be careful not to use too much. Most recipes in this book will call for gluten flour, simply because it is easier to guarantee success with it. Just be aware that if your wheat has been tested out by a good miller, you may not need any gluten flour. Try your wheat flour first by itself in your recipe. Then decide whether or not to add gluten flour. If you choose to use gluten flour, the general rule, as indicated above, is 3–4 tablespoons of gluten flour per loaf of finished bread.

Gluten flour may be found in many grocery stores, most health food stores, bakeries, wheat outlets, or mill shops.

Dough Enhancer

Dough enhancer does just what the name says—it enhances the quality of bread dough. The wheat or wheat flour you use is by far the most important ingredient contributing to successful bread making. It can determine up to 90 percent of your success. Dough enhancer is not a major contributor to product success, but can add a small boost to texture and flavor.

Dough enhancer may contain any combination of whey, ascorbic acid or vitamin C, salt, cornstarch, lecithin, tofu, and flavorings (as well as other ingredients). Whey and tofu provide additional food for the yeast. Vitamin C, or ascorbic acid, repairs and strengthens gluten strands in the dough, and helps counteract the effects of glutathione. Lecithin acts as an emulsifying agent and an antioxidant.

Of all the components of dough enhancers, the most beneficial component is usually the vitamin C, or ascorbic acid. If you just want to minimize glutathione damage in your bread dough, and you want to make bread without the added expense of dough enhancer, you can add just the vitamin C to your bread dough. The next section will explain how.

Ascorbic Acid

Ascorbic acid, or vitamin C, helps sustain the leavening of bread loaves during baking. Ascorbic acid also helps counteract the negative effects of wheat germ. As was mentioned earlier, wheat germ (and active dry yeast, to a small degree) contains a reducing agent called glutathione. This agent breaks down gluten in wheat bread (after you've worked so hard to develop it). Ascorbic acid will not only help prevent the gluten from breaking down, but will help to repair gluten bonds that have already been broken. The benefits of ascorbic acid are more pronounced when flour is low in protein.

When you allow bread dough to rise more than one time, the glutathione in the wheat germ (and possibly the yeast) has more opportunity to work against the gluten in the dough. If you are going to allow your bread dough to rise more than one time, be sure to add ascorbic acid to your bread recipe.

The easiest way to use ascorbic acid is to buy it in powdered form and just measure it directly from the container. However, the least expensive way is to purchase it in tablet form (25–50 mg. tablets), and then mill it right along with your flour.

For a large bread recipe that calls for 24 cups of flour, add 50–200 mg. of ascorbic acid to the flour in the recipe (use the larger amount if you are using active dry or non-instant yeast). If you make a small batch of bread (two loaves), add 15–50 mg. of ascorbic acid.

Lemon juice contains a small amount of ascorbic acid, and there are those who use it in bread dough for that reason. To get enough ascorbic acid from lemon juice to do any good in the bread, a person would need to use 3 ½ cups of lemon juice per batch of bread! Ascorbic acid powder or tablets are much more efficient.

A small amount of lemon juice or vinegar in bread dough can be used to acidify the water in the recipe (½ teaspoon per loaf of bread). Chemical testing is usually needed to determine if the Ph balance needs to be altered.

Whey

Whey is a dairy by-product rich in protein and high in milk sugar. It sweetens the dough slightly, provides extra food for the yeast, and aids browning in the oven. Add whey to your wheat bread if you want a lighter, more delicate color of bread. Add ¼ to ⅓ cup of whey per loaf.

Because dairy whey is also rich in minerals and salts, it can sometimes react inconsistently in bread dough. As was mentioned earlier, watch for unusual results in your bread making when using whey, and use it with care.

Eggs

Eggs enhance whole wheat bread in several ways. As mentioned earlier, lecithin may be used in wheat bread for the binding quality it has on bread dough. In the absence of lecithin, one egg per loaf of bread will act on bread in the same way (lecithin occurs naturally in egg yolks).

Eggs also add a rich golden color to bread, while improving the texture. Eggs also cause bread to rise higher and stay fresh longer. To use eggs, just add the number of eggs called for to a liquid measuring cup, and then add enough liquid to equal the liquid requirement.

Potatoes

It may seem a little unusual that I would include potatoes as an optional ingredient in whole wheat bread. Actually, potatoes are a good source of yeast food, as well as vitamin C.

When cooked, mashed, then added to bread dough, potatoes act as a dough enhancer. Does the name "Spudnuts™" ring a bell? The original Spudnut™ doughnuts contained just that—good old spuds. Do you remember how light and fluffy those doughnuts were? When added to wheat bread, mashed potatoes really do make lighter, better-textured bread. ¼ cup of mashed potatoes per loaf may be added.

If the mashed potatoes are the same consistency as table-ready mashed potatoes, the liquid in the recipe should stay constant. If the potatoes are a little runny, decrease the water by 2 tablespoons for each ¼ cup of mashed potatoes.

You may be tempted to use potato flakes or granules in place of mashed potatoes. Neither of these will have the same beneficial effect as freshly cooked potatoes.

Diastatic and Non-diastatic Malts (Barley, Triticale, etc.)

I mention these malts, not to encourage their use, but

to dispel myths about their use. Barley or other malts may be used as sweetening agents in bread. There are other uses for malts in bread too. However, they may have enzymes present that damage starches or proteins in bread. Professional bakers use various malts, but they also have the proper testing equipment to ensure the results they want. There are enough variables to address when using malts that I discourage their use in homemade wheat bread until a tried and tested product is available for home use.

Using optional ingredients can improve the quality and texture of homemade bread, but the cost per loaf increases. Experiment with these optional ingredients and judge for yourself if the benefit is worth the additional cost.

Hand Mixing and Kneading

Bread making is truly an art for those who choose to make bread the old fashioned way—by hand. There is a wonderfully therapeutic effect when you work your hands through bread dough, making sure by feeling, working, and molding the dough, just when the gluten is perfectly developed. Life seems to be a little richer when we take the time to feel, enjoy, and immerse ourselves in the process, rather than constantly hurrying to just get it done.

You may make bread by hand only because you have no bread mixer. Fortunately, the process is enjoyable and relaxing. You also have the advantage of being able to tell if your dough is kneaded enough by really working with it, and not just looking at it. You will also have peace of mind and pride in your ability to make good bread by hand.

When making bread without an electric or manual bread mixer, a few simple tips can ensure success.

If the recipe calls for 6–8 cups of flour, add only 4–5 cups flour at first. Then add only enough flour while kneading to keep the dough from sticking to the kneading surface and to your hands. The amount of flour used will vary according to humidity in the air, moisture content in the flour, and the type flour used. If the air is humid, you may need more flour. If you live in a dry climate and your flour is very dry, you may need less flour.

If too much flour is added while kneading, the dough will be very hard to handle. The resulting bread will be dry and crumbly. There have been times when I could tell that my dough was too dry, and I tried to add more water after I had been kneading for a few minutes. It's very hard to get the water incorporated again by hand, so be very careful as you begin adding flour—do not add too much too soon.

Kneading becomes easier if you develop a rhythm as you knead. As the dough is worked, it will become smooth on the outside surface. Avoid tearing or breaking through this surface. It will damage the gluten strands that are developing.

Firmly pushing the dough brings the best results. Pounding the dough with a mallet is another way to develop the gluten. Dough has been kneaded enough when it is smooth, satiny, and elastic to the touch. It will generally take 10–15 minutes of good, hard kneading to develop the gluten in the flour properly.

Many batches of bread (including my own first few batches) result in very crumbly bread because the dough has not been kneaded enough. The higher the protein

content of your flour, the longer it takes to develop gluten during the kneading process. Twelve percent protein flour may only take 10 minutes of kneading, while 14 percent protein flour may take 13–14 minutes.

Knead by folding dough and pushing away with the heel of your hand, developing a quick rocking motion. Turn dough a quarter turn, repeating until gluten is developed.

Remember to add gluten flour to your bread recipe if you find that you aren't able to knead the bread dough long enough to develop the gluten sufficiently.

During the kneading process, if the dough seems stiff and hard to handle instead of pliable and elastic, pick it up and throw it onto the kneading surface a few times. It will relax the dough, and you'll spend less time kneading.

After kneading bread dough, there is a quick and easy test that will tell you if the gluten has been adequately developed. Take ½ cup of dough and stretch it gently until you can see light through it. If it tears easily while stretching, the gluten is underdeveloped. If the dough holds together without tearing, the gluten is properly developed.

Machine Mixing and Kneading

When using a bread mixer to mix and knead your

dough, it takes a few batches of bread to become familiar with your machine. For instance, some bread mixers knead the dough so rapidly that if you are not careful, your dough will be completely kneaded before you've had time to add all the flour needed in the recipe. So go slowly with your mixer at first as you become familiar with how it works.

Choose a recipe and follow the recipe instructions for putting the ingredients together. When all the ingredients have been added in your mixer, along with about one-half of the flour, turn the machine on low speed, blending the ingredients together.

If you are making only 2 or 3 loaves of bread, you'll need to add only about ½ cup of flour at a time as the dough mixes. If you are making 5 or 6 loaves, you may add 1 cup of flour at a time as the dough mixes. Keep adding flour, a little at a time, until the dough begins to pull away from the sides of the mixing bowl. Stop adding flour for a moment, until all the existing flour is well incorporated into the dough. Stop the machine if necessary and feel the dough. If the dough holds its shape when a small handful is carefully pulled out of the bowl, it is ready to knead without adding more flour. If the dough is still very sticky,

and seems to slide down the center post of the mixing bowl, then it needs more flour.

When the dough pulls almost completely away from the bowl, it means that the gluten is developing, and is just about the right texture. If your machine is a heavy-duty mixer, allow it to knead until the dough is smooth and elastic.

Remember, too, that the bran in wheat flour absorbs liquid slowly. It may take a few minutes of kneading for the wheat bran to absorb all the liquid that it is going to absorb. Don't add your flour so quickly that the dough becomes too dry when it finally absorbs all the liquid.

If your machine begins to labor, you will know that too much flour has been added to your dough, making it stiff and dry. This is not only hard on the bread mixer, but your finished bread will be compact, heavy, dry, and crumbly.

If the dough is not too stiff, but your machine begins to labor, if may be that your machine is not heavy or big enough to knead the dough completely. You can remove the dough from the mixer and continue kneading it by hand on a smooth surface that has been lightly coated with flour. When the dough is smooth and shiny, the gluten is fully developed.

If you allow your bread mixer to knead too long, the dough will begin to tear instead of stretch as it kneads. At this point, the gluten has been damaged and cannot be repaired. The dough will tear easily as it is formed into loaves, and it will not rise as high as it should.

Once the dough is kneaded, let it rest for 5–10 minutes before molding it into loaves. If it needs to rise once before the loaves are formed, it may be placed in a sprayed bowl immediately and covered with a dry or a damp towel.

Bread on the Rise

You may now see one dilemma that whole wheat bread makers face. The full, rich flavor of wheat bread is achieved by allowing for 2 or more fermentation (rising) periods. Also, gluten is developed further by more than one rising period. Yet, when gluten (that has just been developed through kneading) is constantly exposed to the glutathione in the wheat germ (and regular yeast if it was used, as well as the sharp edges of the bran) during these rising periods, it breaks down, and the bread may become compact and heavy. You end up with a brick that is very flavorful!

I believe that whole wheat bread is the very best (con-sidering all the variables) when it has only one or, at most, two rising periods. Although the flavor may get better with more than two rising periods, the loft and lightness of the loaf can gradually decrease with each rising period. When machine kneading, one rising period (in the bread pans) is enough. When hand kneading, a second rising allows further gluten development.

If you make bread that needs only one rising period in the pans, remember to keep the dough warm (68–82 degrees) while rising (although it will probably still be sufficiently warm from the kneading). However, if temperatures are too warm (above 100 degrees) while rising in the pans, the dough may rise too rapidly, causing the finished loaves to be dense at the bottom and crumbly at the top.

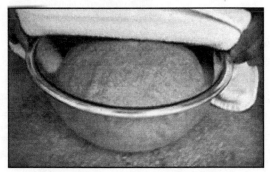

If you make bread that you are going to allow to rise more than once, place the kneaded dough in a large bowl that has been lightly sprayed. Lightly spray the top of the dough also, and then cover it with a dry or damp cloth, depending on the type crust you desire (this is explained in more detail on page 33). Make sure that it is placed in a draft-free location. Place dough in sprayed bowl, then lightly spray top of dough. Cover and let rise until doubled in size (anywhere from 45–90 minutes).

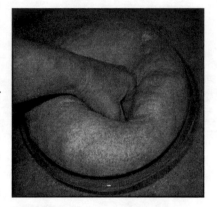

After the dough has risen until it has doubled in size, you can test the dough to see if it is ready to be punched down. Push your index finger about two inches into the dough (very quickly). If the hole you've made stays in the dough without filling in, the dough is ready to punch down. If the hole closes in a little, the dough is not ready. It needs a little more time to ferment. Use this test only on the first rising. Punch down in center, pull edges in. Let rest 10 minutes.

If the dough completely collapses when you test it with your finger, it has risen too long. In fact, if dough is allowed to rise too high at any stage of the bread making process, the bread will collapse on itself and will not rise again. The damage is irreparable. Bread will be crumbly, will smell of alcohol, and will be heavy (thus the term "hard as a brick"). You will be better off starting over again with new ingredients.

Once dough has risen enough, it needs to be punched down. Gently push your fist down into the center of the dough. Then pull the edges of the dough in toward the center. Punch down the dough that is left around the edges, and then turn the dough over. Let it rest for a few minutes. It may then be shaped and placed in sprayed bread pans.

Saving Dough for Later Use

While making bread, you may find that you have to leave your bread making unexpectedly. Bread dough may be refrigerated any time after it has been kneaded and before it is baked. If left for only an hour or two, the bread will probably be fine. If left overnight, the yeast will use up most of its food and the wheat germ will further break down the gluten. The bread will be more compact and heavy after baking, but heavy bread is better than no bread!

Make sure that the dough is punched down well, and then place it in a large bowl that has been lightly sprayed with PAM™. Cover it tightly with plastic wrap and place it in the back of the refrigerator until you are able to finish making bread. You will have to punch the dough down several times if it stays in the refrigerator overnight. Do not save the dough more than one day. When it comes out of the refrigerator, it will take several hours to come up to room temperature. After the dough warms for several hours, mold it into loaves and place it into greased or sprayed pans to rise. If the dough is going to rise at all, it may take several more hours for the dough to rise enough to bake.

SHAPING THE LOAVES

After the dough is punched down from the first rising period, it needs to rest for about 10 minutes before being shaped into loaves. This gives the dough time to relax, and it is much easier to shape the loaves.

There are several ways to shape the dough. One way is to gently divide the bread dough with a serrated knife (without tearing the dough) into the number of loaves you plan to make. If you have a kitchen scale, you can weigh the dough for each loaf. Each ball of dough should weigh 1 ¾ pounds (1 lb. 12 oz.) if you are using standard size pans, or 2 pounds for cast iron or clay pans.

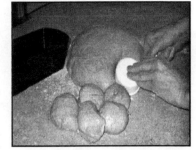

If you do not have a kitchen scale, you may use a clear plastic one cup size measuring cup with a long handle on it to gently divide out 1 cup size pieces of dough from the larger dough mass (lightly spray the measuring cup first). It will take 3 of these measured balls of dough to form a standard loaf of wheat bread, or 3 ½ for cast-iron and clay pans.

If desired, you may use a one-half cup size measuring cup to divide out 6 smaller balls of dough. That will fill a pan with 1 ¾ lbs. of dough. Seven balls of dough will fill a larger pan with 2 lbs. of dough. Some measuring cups are easier to use than others; try your own and decide if you want to use the ½ cup measure or the 1 cup measure. Break out pieces of dough using a plastic measuring cup with a long handle.

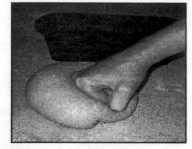

Another way to shape the dough is to place the dough for each loaf on a lightly sprayed counter. For each loaf of bread, pound the dough with your fist into a tight ball to eliminate air bubbles. Then place the ball of dough in the center of a sprayed pan, and cover it with a towel. Even though you are pounding the dough into a ball, take care that you do not tear the dough.

After measuring the amount of dough needed for each loaf, take the pre-measured dough and roll it out on a slightly sprayed or oiled counter into a rectangle, 7½ by 10 inches. Dough can be rolled to the same width as the bread pan. Then roll

the narrow end up, jelly-roll fashion, pinching the seam together. Roll dough up, jelly-roll fashion, pinching seam together. Place the dough into a sprayed pan and cover it with a damp towel.

Never use vegetable oil to coat your bread pans, especially if they are aluminum. The bread might bake right on to the pan! Place dough in center of pan, seam down. Cover and allow to rise until the loaf is doubled in size.

Some people have good luck just breaking out a chunk of dough, smoothing out the top, and placing it in a sprayed pan. I don't seem to have very good luck with this method—I always end up with oddly shaped bread. Sometimes when I am in a hurry, and this is my only option, it may be quite humorous to see what my finished loaves look like, both inside and out.

By the time the dough begins to rise again in the pans, the dough will be cooler than during the first rising period. If the dough is too cool, the dough may not rise well and the loaves will stay compact. A towel may be folded and placed directly beneath the bread pans. This helps insulate the dough.

Also, a warm, light, damp towel may be placed over the top of the rising dough (not only does the warmth help the dough to rise better, but the dampness gives a nice texture to the finished crust). Understandably, the warm towel does cool

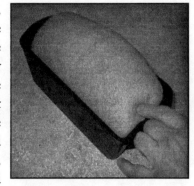

off to room temperature, but does still retain moisture in the loaf. If desired, a dry towel can be used. The crust will just be a little drier.

There is a way to test the dough in the pans to see if it is oven ready. Press your index finger into the dough at the edge of the loaf, next to the pan. Do not press in more than one-fourth inch. If the dent fills back in immediately, the bread is not ready to bake. If the dent very slowly returns to normal, or almost normal, the bread is ready to bake. If the dent does not fill in, the dough has risen too long, and the bread may collapse in the oven. Generally,

you can also tell if your loaves are oven-ready by looking at them. They will be about double in size, and the dough will have risen just above the top of the pan.

VARYING CRUST TEXTURES

For a shiny, chewy crust, dissolve 1 teaspoon corn-starch in ⅔ cup water and bring to a boil. Let it cool slightly, then brush on loaves before baking. Repeat after the first 10 minutes of baking.

For a golden crust, brush loaves with a beaten egg just before baking.

For a crust with seeds, brush the loaves with beaten egg white. Then sprinkle with sesame seeds, poppy seeds, dill seeds, rolled oats, or sunflower seeds. Egg whites by themselves also give a shiny finish.

BAKING, COOLING, AND SLICING BREAD

Whole wheat bread should bake at 375 degrees for about 45 minutes in the center of the oven (unless you live above 4000 feet—see below). Because wheat bread is brown to begin with (or at least darker than white bread), it sometimes will get too brown in the oven. If you like the crust on your wheat bread a little lighter, cover the loaves with aluminum foil (shiny side up) during the last 15–20 minutes of baking.

A well-formed loaf of bread can suddenly develop an uneven shape while baking, because of uneven oven heat. A crack can develop along one side, or the loaf will hang over one side of the pan. The crack will develop on the side which has the lowest oven temperature. Make sure that there is a space between the loaves in the oven so that the heat can circulate evenly between loaves.

Altitude and Climate Adjustments

At altitudes above 4000 feet, there is less atmospheric pressure pushing down against bread dough. Consequently, it takes less time for dough to rise. Bread dough has to bake at a higher temperature initially to quickly stop the dough from rising too high in the oven. At altitudes above 4000 feet, bake wheat bread at 400 degrees for 10 minutes, then at 350 degrees for 25 more minutes.

The recipes in this book were formulated at 4500 feet above sea level. If you live below this level, add 25 percent more yeast and bake the bread at 375 degrees for 40–45 minutes. If you live above 4500 feet, you may need to use less yeast.

If you live in a dry climate, less flour may be needed; in a moist climate, more flour may be needed. Be willing to experiment a little.

Cooling Bread

When bread comes out of the oven, it needs to come out of the pans within five minutes. Otherwise, the bread may become soggy underneath. The loaves may be brushed with melted butter, margarine, or heavy cream while still hot. This leaves a soft, shiny crust. Cool on a rack, and then put away in clean plastic bread sacks.

Hot bread may be dashed quickly under running water. Steam will be created, leaving a soft crust. Another way to create a soft crust is to cool the bread for only 5–10 minutes. Place in a plastic bread sack with the end open to allow excess steam to escape. When the bread is cool, remove it from the plastic sack, wipe excess moisture off the bread with a clean towel, and then place in a clean, dry bread sack. Plastic bread sacks can be found sometimes at day-old bread stores. They can also be found at kitchen specialty shops.

Whole wheat bread will stay fresh for two days at room temperature, two or three days in a refrigerator or up to three months in a freezer (if well wrapped).

Slicing Bread

Slicing your bread can be a mouth-watering experience, or it may be a miserable trial. The knife you use will be the deciding factor. The best knife to use when slicing bread is a long, sharp serrated knife. If you keep your bread knife for slicing bread, and nothing else, it will stay sharp for a long time.

If your bread is still hot when you slice it, your slices need to be a little thicker than normal because the cell walls of the bread are very fragile until the bread cools. Be gentle with the knife. Use a sawing action, going back and forth at least 7 or 8 times before reaching the bottom of the loaf. Try to slice without pushing down too hard on the loaf.

Once the bread has cooled, it is still important to use a sharp, serrated knife. The bread isn't as fragile, but you'll still have better luck slicing with a good knife.

Bread Maker Instructions (Single Loaves)

An automatic bread maker is wonderfully convenient for bread making, but it is not totally automatic when making 100 percent whole wheat bread. It is wise to check the dough as it mixes and rises because more flour may be needed, or more liquid. The dough might rise too high and need a little air punched out of it at the top before baking.

Also, most bread makers are programmed to make white bread. Whole wheat bread may need a longer kneading time, or a longer rising time than white bread. We'll go over these variables that need to be addressed so that the necessary adjustments can be made.

Performance Testing

If you decide to make whole wheat bread in your machine, use wheat flour that has already performed well for you in making bread in your oven. This is probably the single most important factor to consider when making wheat bread in a bread maker.

Measurement Of Ingredients

In my large bread mixer, I can make one loaf of bread or six loaves. My machine is large enough for a lot of variation. In comparison, a bread maker is limited in size, and there isn't much room for fluctuations in measurements. This is why most bread-makers come equipped with measuring utensils. If even ½ cup too much flour is used or ½ teaspoon too much yeast, the bread may not turn out.

The best way to ensure correct measuring is to use a kitchen scale to weigh your ingredients. With a little practice, you'll know exactly how much flour and liquid to use—especially if you use the same type wheat for each loaf.

If you do not have a small kitchen scale, at least try to use accurate measuring utensils each time you bake in your bread maker (also use the same type of wheat each time). If you happen to use freshly-milled wheat flour, and you do not have a kitchen scale, tap each cupful of flour on the counter a few times in order for the flour to settle. Then add another spoonful or two of flour to make the full cup measurement.

Freshly milled flour has a lot of air in it, and if it isn't tapped down a little, it will give you less flour in your recipe than is actually needed. I've had more than one loaf of bread fall because it was short on flour, even though I thought I had measured accurately. Be sure that you don't tap the flour down too much; you may end up with too much flour. Two to three taps on the counter should be plenty.

When using even the most exact measurements, you may look into your bread maker during the kneading process and see your dough just going around and around in a little ball on top of the kneading arm. The dough is too dry and needs more liquid. Add a tablespoonful of water at a time while the dough is kneading until the dough is pliable enough to be kneading instead of just spinning around (it takes a few minutes for the water to incorporate—be patient). If it takes very long to get the dough to a good consistency, you may need to start the kneading process again. Gluten just doesn't develop well in a spin!

At times I have been very exact in my measurements, yet after five minutes of kneading, the dough in the bread maker is still too sticky. Add ¼ cup of flour at a time until the dough is a better texture (it takes time and experience to figure out what a good-textured dough looks like in your machine; be persistent).

Overnight Timing

When using your timer for overnight baking, measure the liquid, salt, sweetener, and oil into the bread maker. Then add flour, optional ingredients, and yeast. The bran in the flour may absorb more moisture than usual because of the extended contact with the water. This can cause your bread to be a little dry. If this happens, add 1–2 tablespoons more liquid to your recipe.

TIME TO DEVELOP GLUTEN

When making white bread in a bread maker, it generally takes 30–35 minutes of kneading to develop the gluten. Because of the bran present in wheat flour, it may take an additional 10–15 minutes of kneading to develop the gluten. It is ideal to have a bread maker that can be programmed to knead for the additional 10–15 minutes. If after trying wheat bread a few times in your bread maker, the gluten just isn't developing enough, you have the option of adding gluten flour to your dough. Three or four tablespoons of gluten flour per 3 cups of wheat flour are usually sufficient.

RISE TIME

Whole wheat bread sometimes needs more time to rise than white bread. In a pre-programmed bread maker, there may not be an allowance for a longer rising cycle. This is the reason for using instant yeast instead of regular, active dry yeast. Instant yeast is more powerful, and can help whole wheat dough rise fast enough in an automatic bread maker

However, make sure that your yeast is fresh, and has been measured correctly. Then make sure that your liquid is barely warm to the touch, and your other ingredients are at room temperature, or a little warmer. This causes your dough to begin rising right after it is kneaded, rather than taking up some of the rise time to get up to room temperature. Some bread makers are equipped with a pre-heating cycle that warms all the ingredients to the ideal temperature before the kneading cycle begins. This can help give all the rise time to the actual rising.

BAKING TIME

In baking white bread, it is relatively easy to regulate the crust color. Because wheat bread is brown even before it is baked, it is common to have bread that is too brown by the time it is baked. Most bread makers allow a choice of light, medium, or dark crust during the baking process. You may want to try baking wheat bread on the light setting.

Notes:
1. "Contribution of Wheat to Human Nutrition." Gur Ranhotra, Ph.D. Director, Nutrition Research, American Institute of Baking, Research Dept. Technical Bulletin vol. XIV, Issue 2, February 1992.
2. "Wheat and Bread: Available Nutrients and Dietary Role." Gur Ranhotra, Ph. D. and Ann Bock, R. D., American

Institute of Baking, Research Dept. Technical Bulletin, Vol. IV, Issue 5, May, 1982.

3. "Wheat Flour Milling." Dale Eustace, Ph. D., Department of Grain Science and Industry, Kansas State University, Manhattan, Kansas. Research Dept. Technical Bulletin, Vol. X, Issue 11, November, 1988.

4. "Nutritive Value of Foods." USDA Home Garden Bulletin No. 72, 1981

5. "Yeast Fermentation in Bread Making." Research Dept. Technical Bulletin, Vol. V, Issue 12, December, 1983. Gary W. Sanderson, Gerald Reed, Bernard Bruinsma, and Elmer J. Cooper, Universal Foods Corporation, Milwaukee, Wisconsin.

CHAPTER 2
Basic Wheat Bread Techniques

Now you are ready to learn the basic method of making whole wheat bread. Read the recipe through twice before starting your bread.

If your flour is lower than 13 percent protein, or if you want extra assurance that your bread will be successful, add the gluten flour that is considered optional.

HAND-KNEADED BREAD TECHNIQUES (2 LOAVES)

As you mill 5–6 cups wheat, measure out liquid into large mixing bowl:

> 3 cups warm water (110 degrees—barely warm to the touch *or*
> 3¼ cups scalded and cooled milk.

If using instant yeast, add 1 ½ tablespoons yeast after the second cup of flour. If using regular yeast, add 2 tablespoons or two packages to water and allow dissolving (5–10 minutes).

Add to warm water or milk:
2 Tbsp. sugar
2 Tbsp. oil *or* 4 tsp. fat
2 tsp. salt
2 cups whole wheat flour
Add yeast, then add 2 more cups flour

Any or all of the following optional ingredients may be added to the recipe, with excellent results:

1 egg (add egg to liquid measuring cup, then add rest of liquid to equal liquid requirement)
6 Tbsp. gluten flour
50 mg. ascorbic acid *or* 4 Tbsp. dough enhancer
½ cup whey
2 Tbsp. molasses *or* honey
½ cup mashed potatoes

1. Stir mixture until smooth. Add 3–4 more cups flour.
2. Knead until smooth, shiny, and satiny, being careful to add only enough flour while kneading to keep dough from sticking to board and hands (10–12 minutes, or approximately 300 kneadings).

Dough that is a little stiff is ideal. Dough that is too soft will fall over the sides of the loaf pans as is rises and bakes.

3. For the quick method, shape dough into 2 loaves, place in sprayed pans, and allow to rise until double. Bake as directed below.
4. For a slower method, place dough into sprayed bowl, then lightly spray the top of the dough. Cover, allowing dough to rise until double. Punch down, allow to rest 10 minutes, then shape into loaves and place into sprayed pans. Allow to rise until doubled in size (cover while rising, if desired, with warm, damp towel).
5. Bake in preheated oven at 400 degrees for 10 minutes, then lower temperature to 350 degrees for 25 minutes.

BREADMIXER BREAD TECHNIQUES (4 LOAVES)

Instructions for use are included with individual bread mixers. Most are similar, but the kneading times may vary. Some bread mixers mix and knead in only 4–5 minutes; some take as long as 10–12 minutes. Be sure to follow the mixing and kneading time for your machine.

> 5¼ cups warm water
> ½ cup honey
> 2 Tbsp. salt
> ¼ cup oil
> 12–15 cups whole wheat flour
> 2½ Tbsp. instant yeast *or* 4 Tbsp. active dry yeast dissolved in ¼ cup of the water measurement

OPTIONAL INGREDIENTS:

Any of the combinations listed below may be added to your bread.

> ¾ cup gluten flour
> ½ cup dough enhancer *or* 60 mg. ascorbic acid
> ½ cup whey powder
> ½ cup molasses (omit honey)
> 1 Tbsp. lecithin

> 3 eggs (put eggs into liquid measuring cup, then add remainder of liquid to equal 5¼ cups)
> 1 cup mashed potatoes

1. Mill approximately 10–11 cups wheat. As it is milling, combine the warm water, oil, honey or molasses, and salt in mixing bowl.
2. Add 7 cups wheat flour, instant yeast (or dissolved regular yeast), and any optional ingredients into the first mixture.
3. Mix together on low speed for 1–2 minutes. Continue adding flour as the machine mixes on low speed (4 more cups, then ½ cup at a time) until the dough is the desired consistency. It takes a few minutes for the wheat flour to absorb the liquid, so add the last of the flour slowly. The dough should be pliable, but not too sticky or too dry.
4. Continue mixing dough on high speed, following mixer manufacturer's directions, until gluten is developed.
5. If desired, the dough may be turned out into a sprayed bowl, covered, and allowed to rise until doubled in size. After dough has doubled, punch

down, place on lightly sprayed counter, and shape into loaves.

6. Step 5 may be omitted, and the dough turned out onto a lightly sprayed counter, kneaded slightly, and divided into loaves or other shapes.

7. Place formed loaves into sprayed pans. Let rise in a warm place, covered with dry or damp towel, until double in size.

8. Bake loaves in a preheated oven at 400 degrees for 10 minutes. Turn oven to 350 degrees and continue baking for 25 more minutes. Cover with aluminum foil the last 20 minutes if necessary, to prevent excess browning.

BREAD MIXER BREAD TECHNIQUES (5–6 LOAVES)

If you have a bread mixer that holds up to 12 pounds of dough, the recipe that follows will utilize the large capacity of the bowl.

7½ cups warm water
¾ cup honey *or* ¾ cup sugar
3 Tbsp. oil
2½ Tbsp. salt
18–22 cups whole wheat flour
2½ Tbsp. instant yeast *or* 4½ Tbsp. active dry yeast, dissolved in ½ cup of the warm water used in the recipe

OPTIONAL INGREDIENTS:

Any of the combinations listed below may be added to your recipe.

1 cup gluten flour
Up to 4 eggs, placed in liquid measuring cup, then rest of liquid added to equal all of liquid
¼ cup molasses
1½ Tbsp. lecithin
100–250 mg. ascorbic acid or ½ cup dough enhancer
1 cup mashed potatoes

1. Mill approximately 15 cups wheat. As it is milling, add the warm water, oil, honey or sugar, and salt together in mixing bowl.
2. Add 10 cups wheat flour, any optional ingredients, and then instant or active dry yeast to the first mixture.
3. Mix together on low speed as more flour is added slowly, 1 cup at a time, until the dough reaches the desired consistency.
4. Continue mixing dough on high speed, following mixer manufacturer's directions, until gluten is developed.
5. Place dough on a lightly sprayed counter, knead slightly, then shape into loaves or other shapes.
6. Dough may be turned out into a sprayed bowl, covered, and allowed to rise until doubled in size.
7. After dough has doubled, punch down, place on slightly sprayed counter, and shape into loaves.
8. Place formed loaves into sprayed pans. Let rise in warm place, covered, until double in size.
9. Bake loaves in preheated oven at 400 degrees for 10 minutes. Turn oven to 350 degrees and continue baking for 25–30 minutes. Cover with aluminum foil the last 20 minutes, if necessary, to prevent excess browning.

French Bread

The secret to good French bread is in the baking. Steam creates a thick, lightly browned, chewy crust. To create steam, a clay baker is perfect. It simulates a brick oven that gives French bread the thick, chewy crust.

Use any of the bread recipes given, omitting oil and sweetener. After the dough is completely kneaded, place dough into a lightly sprayed bowl, cover, and allow to rise until double.

1. Punch down carefully, then let rest for 10 minutes. Divide dough into 3 cup portions.
2. Follow the instructions below to either make round loaves, oblong loaves, twisted oblong loaves, or braided loaves.
3. Bake in a preheated oven at 425 degrees for 10 minutes, then at 350 degrees for 25 more minutes.
4. For round loaves, pound dough into a tight ball. Place in center of lightly sprayed round cast iron skillet, or a round pizza pan that has been sprinkled with corn meal. After dough has doubled in size, lightly score the top of the dough with a serrated knife dipped in water. Score twice across and twice down, creating slanted lines.
5. For oblong loaves, roll each portion into an 8 x 16 inch rectangle. Roll up the short way, creating a long roll. Use a rolling pin to slightly flatten the loaf. Place on sprayed cookie sheet that has been lightly sprinkled with corn meal. After rising until doubled in size, slash across the dough with serrated, wet knife, about 5 times.
6. For a twisted oblong loaf, follow step 4 above. After rolling the dough into an oblong shape, let it rest 5–10 minutes. Twist the dough two full turns, then place on a sprayed cookie sheet. After rising until doubled in size, brush with beaten egg white, and sprinkle with sesame seeds.
7. For a braided loaf, roll 2–3 cups of dough out as long as the pan you will use. Roll 9 inches wide. With a pizza cutter, cut the 9 inches into 3 long strips each 3 inches wide by the length of the pan. Roll each strip up lengthwise, forming 3 long ropes. Pinch the 3 strips together at the top. Braid them into a thick braid, tucking the ends under at

the bottom. Brush with egg white, sprinkle with sesame seeds, and place in sprayed clay baker or out on a sprayed cookie sheet. Let rise until doubled in size.

Pita Bread

1. Make any of the bread recipes given, omitting oil and/or lecithin. Make certain that your dough is a soft dough, and not dry and hard.
2. Allow dough to rest for 10 minutes after kneading. Break out ½ cup size portions of dough. Form balls, cover with clean towel, and let stand 15 minutes.
3. Preheat oven to 475 degrees. The oven must be completely warmed, because this creates the pocket.
4. Roll each ball on a floured surface to ½ inch thickness. Place on an ungreased cookie sheet that has been sprinkled with ¼ cup cornmeal. If you are making a large recipe, place on counter that is sprinkled with cornmeal. When you are ready to bake, move gently with fingers to cookie sheet.
5. Allow to rise for a full half hour.
6. Bake on lowest rack of oven for 5–10 minutes, or until puffed up and turning brown.
7. Remove from oven and allow to cool completely. Store in closed plastic bags in refrigerator, or freeze for longer storage.

PITA BREAD HELPFUL HINTS:

A. The basic plan in making pita bread is to get steam to puff up inside the bread before the bread bakes. This is why you need soft, moist dough with no fat in it. Also, this is why the bread is baked at a very high temperature at the bottom of the oven.
B. If your bread is burning on the bottom before it can puff up, try putting your cookie sheet on the next to bottom shelf of the oven with the oven turned up to 500 degrees .
C. Thick cookie sheets may not allow heat to penetrate quickly enough to the pita bread dough. This will cause the bread to cook before it has a chance to puff up. Thin cookie sheets work better for pita bread.

Rolls, Buns, and Breadsticks

Cinnamon Rolls (10–15 rolls)

1. Use any of the bread mixer recipes. Add an extra ½ cup of sugar if desired, to make a sweeter dough.
2. On a lightly sprayed counter, roll 6 cups of dough into a 12 x 16 inch rectangle. Spread dough with 6 Tbsp. melted butter or margarine.
3. Spread with a mixture of 1 cup white or brown sugar and 2 teaspoons cinnamon.
4. Sprinkle with 1 cup coarsely chopped walnuts or pecans (1 cup raisins are optional).
5. Roll up and seal ends. Use dental floss or serrated knife to cut the dough into 1½ inch wide rolls. Flatten the rolls slightly onto 2 or 3 sprayed cookie sheets.
6. Cover and let rise 45–60 minutes. Bake in a preheated oven at 375 degrees for 20–25 minutes. Frost when cool.

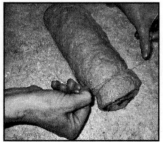

FROSTING FOR CINNAMON ROLLS

    4 cups powdered sugar
    6 Tbsp. butter
    1 tsp. vanilla
    3–6 Tbsp. milk or cream

Mix sugar, butter, and vanilla together. Add milk or cream gradually until frosting is smooth and spreads easily.

VARIATIONS:

A. Substitute ½ to 1 teaspoon of almond or maple flavoring for the vanilla.
B. Substitute 3 oz. cream cheese for 3 tablespoons of the butter.
C. Add ½ teaspoon coconut flavoring to frosting and sprinkle frosted cinnamon rolls with shredded coconut.

Sometimes, nuts or raisins, combined with the melted butter will cause a space between the rounds of the cinnamon roll. It helps to place the cinnamon rolls on the sprayed pan so they touch or almost touch before they rise. Then they have to rise upward, forcing the rolls to form a tighter network of dough.

Dinner Rolls (24 rolls)

1. Use any of the bread mixer recipes, adding 3 eggs to the ingredients (add to liquid requirement).
2. Add ¼ cup butter to ingredients.
3. Break out 6 cups of dough.
4. Place dough on lightly sprayed counter and break out ½ cup size pieces of dough. Divide each in half again, pound into a small ball, and place on a sprayed cookie sheet. An average size cookie sheet holds 20–24 dinner rolls.
5. Cover and let rise in warm place until double. Bake in preheated oven at 375 degrees for 20 minutes.
6. If there is dough from the recipe left over, it can be formed into loaves, or rolled out to ½ inch thickness, cut in desired shapes, and fried in butter.

Breadsticks (makes about 2 dozen)

1. Use any of the bread mixer recipes. Roll 3 cups dough to ½ inch thickness. Spread with melted butter or beaten egg white. Sprinkle with Parmesan cheese or sesame seeds.
2. Cut dough down center with pizza cutter. Then cut strips across 1–2 inches wide.
3. Twist bread sticks if desired, or lay straight on sprayed cookie sheet.
4. Cover and allow to rise for 30–45 minutes. Bake in preheated oven at 375 degrees for 15 minutes.

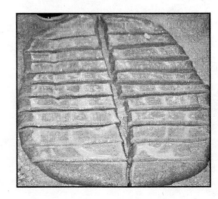

Hamburger Buns (8–12 buns)

1. Using any of the basic bread recipes given, roll 3 cups of dough to ¾ inch thickness. Cut circles of desired size and transfer to sprayed cookie sheet. A wide-mouth thermos lid works well or wide-mouth gallon lid.
2. If desired, brush tops with beaten egg white and sprinkle with sesame seeds.
3. Cover and allow to rise until doubled in size. Bake in preheated oven at 375 degrees for 20–25 minutes.

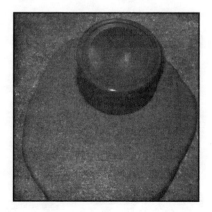

Hot Dog or Hoagie Buns (8–12 buns)

1. Using any of the bread mixer recipes, roll 3 cups of dough to ½ inch thickness. Cut circles of desired size. Fold circle in half and stretch to elongate (I found a thin metal cookie cutter, which I reshaped to make a hot dog shaped cutter). You may also use the top cover of a butter dish.
2. Place on sprayed cookie sheet.
3. Cover and allow to rise until doubled in size. Bake in preheated oven at 375 degrees for 23 minutes.

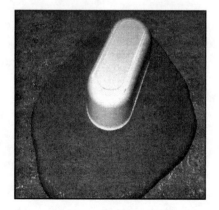

Automatic Bread Maker Techniques

Dough Setting

Any recipe desired can be mixed on the dough setting. When the dough cycle is complete, the dough can be removed from the machine, and used for rolls, breadsticks, hamburger, or hot dog buns.

The bread maker basic recipe section would not be complete, however, without a recipe for cinnamon rolls. Following is a mouth-watering version especially for whole wheat enthusiasts.

Bread Maker Cinnamon Rolls (4–10 rolls)

White wheat flour allows the cinnamon, brown sugar, and butter flavors to be more pronounced. Either scald the milk and cool before using, or use warm evaporated milk.

	LARGE	MEDIUM	SMALL
DOUGH:			
warm milk	⅔ cup	½ cup	⅓ cup
warm water	½ cup	⅜ cup	¼ cup
eggs	2	1	1
salt	1 tsp.	¾ tsp.	½ tsp.
sugar	3 Tbsp.	2¼ Tbsp.	1½ Tbsp.
melted butter	¼ cup	3 Tbsp.	2 Tbsp.
wheat flour	3¼ cups	2¼ cups	1½ cups
gluten flour	3 Tbsp.	2 Tbsp.	1½ Tbsp.
instant yeast	1¼ tsp.	1 tsp.	½ tsp.
FILLING:			
melted butter	½ cup	6 Tbsp.	¼ cup
sugar	½ cup	6 Tbsp.	¼ cup
cinnamon	1 Tbsp.	2 tsp.	1½ tsp.
brown sugar	½ cup	6 Tbsp.	¼ cup
chopped nuts	1 cup	¾ cup	½ cup
raisins (opt.)	½ cup	⅓ cup	¼ cup

ICING:

powdered sugar	2 cups	1½ cups	1 cup
corn syrup	2 Tbsp.	1½ Tbsp.	1 Tbsp.
orange juice	¼ cup	3 Tbsp.	2 Tbsp.

Soak raisins in hot water until plump. Drain. Add dough ingredients to bread maker. Select dough cycle. When cycle is complete, take dough and roll out on a floured surface into a 7½ x 10 inch rectangle. Brush dough with melted butter. Combine rest of filling ingredients except raisins and sprinkle on dough. Finish with the raisins and roll jelly roll fashion, starting with long edge. Seal edges, slice into 5–12 rolls, depending upon the size of your bread maker recipe. Place cut side down onto sprayed baking sheet. Cover and let rise in a warm place until doubled in size (at least one hour, possibly as much as two hours). Bake in a preheated 350 degree oven for 20–25 minutes. Remove from oven, brush with melted butter, and drizzle with icing.

Basic Whole Wheat Bread (1 loaf)

	LARGE	MEDIUM	SMALL
lukewarm water	1½ cups	1⅛ cups	¾ cup
lecithin	1½ tsp.	1 tsp.	¾ tsp.
oil	1½ Tbsp.	1 Tbsp.	2½ tsp.
salt	1½ tsp.	1 tsp.	¾ tsp.
sugar or honey	2 Tbsp.	1½ Tbsp.	1 Tbsp.
wheat flour	3¼ cups	2¼ cups	1½ cups
gluten flour	3 Tbsp.	2⅓ Tbsp.	1½ Tbsp.
instant yeast	1¼ tsp.	¾ tsp.	½ tsp.

OPTIONAL INGREDIENTS:

	LARGE	MEDIUM	SMALL
dough enhancer	1½ tsp.	1 tsp.	¾ tsp.
ascorbic acid	25 mg.	20 mg.	15 mg.
molasses	2 Tbsp.	1½ Tbsp.	1 Tbsp.

Measure the water first into the bread maker. Then measure the other ingredients in the order given, with the yeast being last. If you desire to use any optional ingredients, measure them before the yeast. Select your setting as outlined in your bread maker instructions. Press the start button and proceed. It may be wise to check the dough after 4–5 minutes of kneading and mixing. If more flour is needed, add it then. Proceed until completed.

CHAPTER 3
Wheat Bread Recipes

The recipes in this section make more than one loaf of bread. For this reason, they are separated from the automated bread maker recipes. However, as you gain more experience in bread making, you may wish to make some of these recipes in a bread maker. Try cutting the ingredients in half, or fourth. Be sure to use the principles of whole wheat bread making, and follow the specific instructions for your automatic bread maker. You may also make any of the following recipes by hand.

Applesauce Bread (3–4 loaves)

This is a healthy bread that tastes great when spread with apple butter.

2 cups warm water or apple juice
2 cups applesauce
½ cup sugar
1½ Tbsp. salt
2 Tbsp. oil

8–11 cups whole wheat flour
1½ Tbsp. instant yeast
½ cup gluten flour

Measure warm water or apple juice into mixing bowl. Add applesauce, sugar, salt, oil, and 7 cups wheat flour. Mix ingredients on low speed. After 1 minute, add yeast and gluten flour. Increase mixer speed while adding remaining flour, ½ cup at a time, until dough pulls away from sides of bowl. Knead until gluten is fully developed (8–9 minutes on low speed, 5–6 minutes on high speed). Turn dough out onto sprayed counter. Mold dough into loaves, place in sprayed bread pans, cover, and let rise until doubled in size. Bake in preheated 400 degree oven for 10 minutes. Lower oven temperature to 350 degrees and continue baking for 25–30 minutes. Cover loaves with aluminum foil the last 15 minutes, if needed, to prevent excess browning.

Buckwheat Bread (4–5 loaves)

5 cups warm water
2 Tbsp. salt
½ cup brown sugar
2 Tbsp. lecithin
2 Tbsp. oil
100 mg. ascorbic acid

2 tsp. maple flavoring
2 cups buckwheat flour
10–12 cups wheat flour
⅔ cup gluten flour
2 Tbsp. instant yeast

Mill 2 cups hulled buckwheat, then measure the 2 cups buckwheat flour. Mill 8–10 cups wheat. Measure 5 cups warm water into mixing bowl. Add salt, sugar, lecithin, oil, ascorbic acid, and maple flavoring. Mix slightly, then add 7 cups wheat flour, 2 cups buckwheat flour, gluten flour, and instant yeast. Mix at low speed while adding 3–5 more cups flour, ½ cup at a time, until dough pulls away from sides of bowl.

Knead dough until gluten is developed. Turn dough out onto sprayed counter. Mold into loaves, place in sprayed pans, cover, and let rise until doubled in size. Bake in preheated 400 degree oven for 10 minutes. Turn heat down to 350 degrees and continue baking for 25–28 minutes until loaves are done. Cover with aluminum foil the last 10 minutes, if needed, to prevent excess browning.

Pinto Bean Bread (4–5 loaves)

Pinto bean bread has a very light texture. It goes well with hearty corn chowder.

5¼ cups warm water
2 cups cooked, mashed pinto beans*
2 Tbsp. salt
2 Tbsp. lecithin
2 Tbsp. oil

½ cup honey
75 mg. ascorbic acid (opt.)
14–17 cups whole wheat flour
¾ cup gluten flour
2 Tbsp. instant yeast

Measure warm water into mixing bowl. Add pinto beans, salt, lecithin, oil, honey, ascorbic acid (opt.), and 7 cups wheat flour. Slowly blend ingredients together on low speed while adding 2 more cups flour, gluten flour, and instant yeast. Increase mixing speed while adding more flour, ½ cup at a time, until dough pulls away from sides of mixing bowl.

Knead until gluten is fully developed. Turn dough out onto lightly sprayed counter. Spray hands lightly. Form dough into loaves, place in sprayed pans, cover, and let rise until doubled in size. Bake in preheated 400 degree oven for 10 minutes. Lower oven temperature to 350 degrees and continue baking for 25–30 minutes. Cover loaves with aluminum foil during last 15 minutes to prevent excess browning.

Canned, refried beans may be used. For quick pinto beans, mill 1½ cups dry pinto beans into flour. Stir it into 3 cups boiling water. Cover and cook over low heat for 5–6 minutes. Remove from heat and allow to cool. Measure out 2 cups for bread.

Pumpernickel Bread (3–4 loaves)

4½ cups warm water
½ cup molasses
1½ Tbsp. lecithin
1½ Tbsp. oil
2 Tbsp. salt
2½ Tbsp. cocoa powder

2 Tbsp. caraway seed
1½ cups rye flour
8–10 cups whole wheat flour
¾ cup gluten flour
2½ Tbsp. instant yeast

Measure warm water into mixing bowl. Add molasses, lecithin, oil, salt, cocoa powder, caraway seed, and rye flour. Begin mixing on low speed while adding 6–7 cups wheat flour. Add gluten flour and yeast. Increase mixer speed, adding remaining flour, ½ cup at a time, until dough pulls away from sides of mixing bowl.

Knead until gluten is fully developed. Turn dough out onto lightly sprayed counter. Form into 3 rounds of dough, pounding each with your fist into a tight, smooth ball. Place each on a sprayed cookie sheet. Cover and allow to rise until doubled in size. Slash the top of each with a serrated knife. Spray with water, and bake in a preheated 350 degree oven for 40 minutes. Cover with aluminum foil for the last 10 minutes, if needed, to prevent excess browning.

Sesame Seed Bread (3–4 Loaves)

3 eggs broken into measuring cup (add warm water to equal 4 cups)
½ cup honey
1 Tbsp. salt
2½ Tbsp. oil
1 cup mashed potatoes (opt.)

¾ cup sesame seeds, divided
9–12 cups whole wheat flour
¾ cup gluten flour
2 Tbsp. instant yeast
1 beaten egg white

Measure warm water, eggs, honey, salt, and oil into the mixing bowl. Then add mashed potatoes, 5 cups wheat flour, gluten flour, yeast and ½ cup of the sesame seeds. Mix together on low speed for 1½ minutes. Add 3 more cups flour and turn mixer to medium speed. Continue adding flour, ½ cup at a time, until dough pulls away from sides of mixing bowl.

Knead until gluten is developed (5–6 minutes at high speed, 8–9 minutes at medium speed). Turn dough out onto lightly oiled or sprayed counter and form into loaves. Spray loaf pans, then sprinkle 1½ teaspoons of sesame seeds into the bottom of each loaf pan. Place formed loaves into pans, on top of sesame seeds. Brush tops of loaves with egg white, then sprinkle 1 teaspoon sesame seeds over the top of each loaf. The sesame seeds will adhere to the egg whites. Cover lightly with a dry cloth and let rise until doubled in size.

Bake in a preheated 400 degree oven for 10 minutes. Turn oven down to 350 degrees and continue baking for 25–30 minutes. Cover with foil for the last 10 minutes, if needed, to prevent excess browning. Remove from oven and cool on racks.

Sunflower-millet Bread (4–5 Loaves)

White wheat flour allows the flavor of the different seeds to be more pronounced.

5½ cups warm water
½ cup sugar
1½ Tbsp. salt
2 Tbsp. oil
2 Tbsp. lecithin
100 mg. ascorbic acid, milled with wheat
2 cups rolled oats (regular or instant)
9–12 cups whole wheat flour

1 cup shelled, raw sunflower seeds
½ cup millet
¾ cup gluten flour
2½ Tbsp. instant yeast
1 beaten egg white
½ cup rolled oats
¼ cup sunflower seeds
3 Tbsp. millet

Measure warm water, sugar, salt, oil, lecithin, and ascorbic acid milled with wheat into mixing bowl. Add oats, 5 cups wheat flour, sunflower seeds, ½ cup millet, gluten flour, and yeast. Mix together on low speed, then add 5 more cups flour. Increase speed to medium, then add flour, ½ cup at a time, until dough pulls away from the sides of the bowl. Knead until gluten is developed.

Turn dough out onto lightly oiled or sprayed counter. Form into loaves, and place into sprayed pans or a round loaf may be formed and placed on a sprayed cookie sheet. Brush tops of loaves with beaten egg white. Sprinkle rolled oats, sunflower seeds, and 3 tablespoons millet on top of loaves. Cover lightly and allow to rise until doubled in size.

Bake in preheated 400 degree oven for 10 minutes. Reduce heat to 350 degrees and bake 25–30 minutes longer. Remove from oven and cool on racks.

Wheat, Corn Bread (4–5 loaves)

This bread resembles the Early American Anadama Bread. Corn flour is used instead of cornmeal, giving a finer texture to the bread. White wheat flour allows the corn flavor to be more pronounced. This bread has a delicate corn flavor, and is delicious with ham and bean stew.

5½ cups warm water
¼ cup molasses
2 Tbsp. honey
2 Tbsp. lecithin
2 Tbsp. oil

2 Tbsp. salt
3 cups corn flour
12–15 cups whole wheat flour
1 cup gluten flour
2½ Tbsp. instant yeast

Measure water, molasses, honey, lecithin, oil, salt, and corn flour into mixing bowl. Add 7 cups wheat flour. Turn bread mixer to low speed. While mixing, add gluten flour and yeast. After 1½ minutes, increase speed of bread mixer and gradually add remaining wheat flour, ½ cup at a time, until dough pulls away from sides of bowl.

Continue kneading until gluten is fully developed. Turn dough out onto a lightly sprayed counter. Shape into loaves, place in sprayed bread pans, cover, and let rise until doubled in size. Bake in preheated oven at 400 degrees for 10 minutes. Turn oven to 350 degrees and continue baking for 25–30 minutes or until done. Cover loaves with aluminum foil for the last 20 minutes to prevent excess browning.

Whole Wheat Pizza Crust (two 12" crusts)

1 egg (add egg to measuring cup, add warm water to equal 2½ cups)
2 tsp. sugar
1 Tbsp. salt
1 Tbsp. softened butter

1½ tsp. Italian seasoning
¼ cup mashed potatoes
5–6 cups whole wheat flour
1 Tbsp. instant yeast
¼ cup gluten flour

Measure water, egg, sugar, salt, butter, Italian seasoning, and mashed potatoes into bread mixer. Add 3 cups wheat flour, gluten flour, and yeast. Mix on low speed for about 1½ minutes. Add 2–3 more cups flour, a little at a time, until dough is firm, but not stiff. It should pull away from the sides of the bowl. Knead for about 5 minutes on medium speed.

When gluten is developed, stop mixer, cover dough, and allow to rise until doubled in size. Turn dough out onto lightly sprayed counter. Divide into two equal balls of dough and let rest for 10 minutes. Spray two, 12" pans with oil. After dough has rested, begin gently stretching one ball of dough into a 12" circle.

Place your hands under the small circle of dough, palms down (dough will be resting on the backs of your hands). Pull your hands apart under the dough (keeping fingers extended), gently stretching the dough. You may want to try gently tossing the dough into the air from the backs of your hands, causing it to twirl in the air. Let it come back down on the backs of your hands. Repeat until dough is basically the size of the pizza pan. Place dough on pan, gently stretching it to fit. Do not roll dough with a pizza roller; it will flatten all the air bubbles that were just created by the twirling. Repeat with the other ball of dough.

Allow the dough to rise until doubled in size. Preheat oven to 450 degrees. Bake crust for 6 minutes. Remove from oven and spread with desired toppings. Return to oven and bake 7–8 more minutes or until cheese melts.

BREAD MAKER RECIPES (single loaves)

The recipes that follow have been formulated especially for automated bread makers. However, any of them may be made in any bread mixer or by hand. The recipes may also be doubled or tripled so that more than one loaf can be made at a time.

Remember that these recipes have been formulated at 4500 feet above sea level. Below this altitude, add 25 percent more instant yeast than is called for in the recipe. Above 5000 feet, use 20 percent less yeast.

If your bread maker has a wheat bread setting (or a programmable setting), always use it for these wheat bread recipes (the exception is if you are using the raisin bread setting or the dough setting). Otherwise, use the white bread setting.

If you like experimenting a little, it is fun to add ½ to 1 cup whole nuts to any recipe (filberts, macadamias, pecans, walnuts, cashews, etc.). Add ½ teaspoon extra yeast for the large loaf, ⅜ teaspoon for the medium loaf, and ¼ teaspoon for the small loaf. Choose the raisin bread setting. When the machine beeps, add the nuts.

If your bread making machine does not have a raisin bread cycle, add the needed ingredients just before the end of the second kneading cycle.

Almond Oat Bread

	LARGE	MEDIUM	SMALL
lukewarm water	1½ cups	1⅛ cups	¾ cup
honey	3 Tbsp.	2¼ Tbsp.	1½ Tbsp.
rolled oats	¾ cup	½ cup	¼ cup
salt	1½ tsp.	1 tsp.	¾ tsp.
softened butter	2½ Tbsp.	2 Tbsp.	1½ Tbsp.
almond flavor	1 Tbsp.	2¼ tsp.	1½ tsp.
wheat flour	3¼ cups	2½ cups	1¾ cups
gluten flour	3 Tbsp.	2¼ Tbsp.	1½ Tbsp.
instant yeast	1¾ tsp.	1¼ tsp.	1 tsp.
slivered almonds	¾ cup	½ cup	6 Tbsp.

Measure lukewarm water into bread maker, followed by remaining ingredients. Add the yeast last, then program the bread maker for raisin bread. At the beep, add the almonds. If desired, omit the almonds, then program the bread maker for wheat or white bread.

Apple Raisin Bread

	LARGE	MEDIUM	SMALL
lukewarm water	1 cup	¾ cup	½ cup
applesauce	½ cup	⅜ cup	¼ cup
salt	1½ tsp.	1⅛ tsp.	¾ tsp.
butter	2 Tbsp.	1½ Tbsp.	1 Tbsp.
brown sugar	2 Tbsp.	1½ Tbsp.	1 Tbsp.
cinnamon	1 tsp.	¾ tsp.	½ tsp.
wheat flour	3 cups	2¼ cups	1½ cups
instant yeast	1½ tsp.	1⅛ tsp.	¾ tsp.
gluten flour	3 Tbsp.	2¼ Tbsp.	1½ Tbsp.
raisins	⅝ cup	½ cup	¼ cup
chopped walnuts or pecans (opt.)	⅝ cup	½ cup	¼ cup

Add ingredients to bread machine in order given, except the raisins and optional nuts. Program the machine for raisin bread. When the machine beeps, add raisins (and nuts if desired). If you choose to use nuts in your bread, increase the yeast by ½ teaspoon for a large loaf, ⅜ teaspoon for a medium loaf, and ¼ teaspoon for a small loaf.

Bacon, Egg, and Cheese Bread

	LARGE	MEDIUM	SMALL
lukewarm water and 1 egg to equal:	1½ cups	1⅛ cups	¾ cup
grated cheese	½ cup	⅜ cup	¼ cup
salt	1½ tsp.	1⅛ tsp.	¾ tsp.
sugar	2 Tbsp.	1½ Tbsp.	1 Tbsp.
butter	2 Tbsp.	1½ Tbsp.	1 Tbsp.
wheat flour	3 cups	2¼ cups	1½ cups
instant yeast	1½ tsp.	1 tsp.	¾ tsp.
gluten flour	3 Tbsp.	2¼ Tbsp.	1½ Tbsp.
bacon (real bits)	4 Tbsp.	3 Tbsp.	2 Tbsp.

Add all ingredients except bacon in the order given. Set the bread maker for the raisin bread option. Add the bacon when the machine beeps.

Buttermilk Cheese Bread

	LARGE	MEDIUM	SMALL
buttermilk (scalded and cooled)	1 cup	¾ cup	½ cup
warm water	½ cup	⅜ cup	¼ cup
grated cheese	1 cup	¾ cup	½ cup
sugar	1 Tbsp.	2¼ tsp.	1½ tsp.
salt	1 tsp.	¾ tsp.	½ tsp.
baking soda	1 tsp.	¾ tsp.	½ tsp.
wheat flour	3 cups	2¼ cups	1½ cups
gluten flour	3 Tbsp.	2¼ Tbsp.	1½ Tbsp.
instant yeast	1½ tsp.	1 tsp.	¾ tsp.

Measure all ingredients into the bread maker in the order given, except for the cheese. Choose the raisin bread setting. When the machine beeps, add the cheese. This bread is great with pasta or pizza.

Buttermilk Wheat Bread

	LARGE	MEDIUM	SMALL
buttermilk (scalded and cooled)	1½ cups	1 cup	¾ cup
softened butter	1 Tbsp.	2 tsp.	1½ tsp.
salt	1½ tsp.	1 tsp.	¾ tsp.
baking soda	1½ tsp.	1 tsp.	¾ tsp.
sugar	2 Tbsp.	1½ Tbsp.	1 Tbsp.
caraway seeds	2 Tbsp.	1½ Tbsp.	1 Tbsp.
wheat flour	3¼ cups	2⅜ cups	1½ cups
instant yeast	1½ tsp.	1 tsp.	¾ tsp.
gluten flour	3 Tbsp.	2¼ Tbsp.	1½ Tbsp.
raisins (opt.)	⅔ cup	½ cup	⅓ cup

Measure ingredients into bread maker in order given. If you use raisins in your recipe, select the raisin bread cycle and add the raisins when the machine beeps. Otherwise, select the wheat bread setting.

Cheddar Cheese Bread

	LARGE	MEDIUM	SMALL
lukewarm water	1⅓ cups	¾ cup	½ cup
sugar	2 Tbsp.	1½ Tbsp.	1 Tbsp.
salt	1 tsp.	¾ tsp.	½ tsp.
egg	1	1	1
softened butter	2 Tbsp.	1½ Tbsp.	1 Tbsp.
wheat flour	3¼ cups	2⅛ cups	1½ cups
black pepper (opt.)	1 tsp.	¾ tsp.	½ tsp.
gluten flour	3 Tbsp.	2¼ Tbsp.	1½ Tbsp.
instant yeast	1½ tsp.	1 tsp.	¾ tsp.

Measure liquid ingredients into bread maker (including egg). Measure the dry ingredients, ending with yeast. Program bread maker to make raisin bread. Begin cycle, then prepare cheese mixture as follows:

cheddar cheese	1 cup	¾ cup	½ cup
wheat flour	2 Tbsp.	1½ Tbsp.	1 Tbsp.

Place flour in plastic bag. Add grated cheese and shake bag, coating cheese with flour. Sift remaining flour out, then add to bread dough when the bread maker beeps. If your machine has no raisin bread cycle, add the cheese during the last two minutes of the second knead cycle.

Chocolate Chip Bread

	LARGE	MEDIUM	SMALL
lukewarm water and 1 egg to equal:	1½ cups	1⅛ cups	¾ cup
brown sugar	5 Tbsp.	3½ Tbsp.	2½ Tbsp.
butter	2 Tbsp.	1½ Tbsp.	1 Tbsp.
salt	1½ tsp.	1⅛ tsp.	¾ tsp.
white wheat flour	3¼ cups	2⅛ cups	1½ cups
gluten flour	3 Tbsp.	2¼ Tbsp.	1½ Tbsp.
instant yeast	1½ tsp.	1⅛ tsp.	¾ tsp.
chocolate chips*	1 cup	¾ cup	½ cup
walnut halves	½ cup	⅓ cup	¼ cup

Place all ingredients into bread maker in order given, except chocolate chips and nuts. Use the raisin bread setting. When machine beeps, add chips and nuts.

Semi-sweet or milk chocolate chips may be used.

Colonial bread is delicious when served with ham and bean soup.

	LARGE	MEDIUM	SMALL
boiling water	1½ cups	1⅛ cups	¾ cup
corn meal	⅓ cup	4 Tbsp.	2¾ Tbsp.
softened butter	1 Tbsp.	2 tsp.	1½ tsp.
sugar	1 Tbsp.	2 tsp.	1½ tsp.
salt	1¼ tsp.	1 tsp.	¾ tsp.
molasses	⅓ cup	4 Tbsp.	2¾ Tbsp.
wheat flour	3 cups	2¼ cups	1½ cups
gluten flour	3 Tbsp.	2¼ Tbsp.	1½ Tbsp.
instant yeast	1½ tsp.	1 tsp.	¾ tsp.

Place cornmeal into bowl. Carefully stir boiling water into cornmeal until it is smooth. Let cool for about 30 minutes. Pour into bread maker, followed by other ingredients in the order given. Start the cycle.

Cracked Wheat Bread

	LARGE	MEDIUM	SMALL
boiling water	½ cup	⅜ cup	¼ cup
cracked wheat	½ cup	⅜ cup	¼ cup
lecithin	2 Tbsp.	1½ Tbsp.	1 Tbsp.
evaporated milk (lukewarm)	1¼ cups	1 cup	½ cup
honey	3 Tbsp.	2¼ Tbsp.	1½ Tbsp.
salt	1½ tsp.	1⅛ tsp.	¾ tsp.
ginger	¼ tsp.	⅛ tsp.	pinch
wheat flour	3½ cups	2¾ cups	¼ cups
gluten flour	3 Tbsp.	2¼ Tbsp.	1½ Tbsp.
instant yeast	1½ tsp.	1 tsp.	¾ tsp.

Cover the ½ cup cracked wheat (crack your own in a blender or purchase it in a health food store) with boiling water in a small bowl. When it is cool, place it in the bread maker, followed by the other ingredients in the order given. Start the cycle.

French Bread

	LARGE	MEDIUM	SMALL
hot water	1 cup	¾ cup	½ cup
softened butter	2 Tbsp.	1½ Tbsp.	1 Tbsp.
salt	1 tsp.	¾ tsp.	½ tsp.
sugar	2 Tbsp.	1½ Tbsp.	1 Tbsp.
wheat flour	3 cups	2¼ cups	1½ cups
gluten flour	3 Tbsp.	2¼ Tbsp.	1½ Tbsp.
instant yeast	1¼ tsp.	1 tsp.	¾ tsp.
egg whites	2	1	1
corn flour	1 Tbsp.	1 Tbsp.	1 Tbsp.

Whip egg whites until stiff, and set aside. Place other ingredients in bread maker in order given. Start the machine on the dough setting. When all the ingredients are moistened, add egg whites. When the cycle is complete, place dough in a round ball on a cookie sheet that has been sprayed, then sprinkled with corn flour. Let rise until doubled in size, slash top, brush with water, and bake in preheated 400 degree oven for 10 minutes. Lower temperature to 350 degrees and bake for an additional 25–30 minutes.

Golden Egg Bread

	LARGE	MEDIUM	SMALL
warm water	1 cup	¾ cup	½ cup
oil	2 Tbsp.	1½ Tbsp.	1 Tbsp.
eggs	2	1	1
sugar	¼ cup	3 Tbsp.	2 Tbsp.
salt	1½ tsp.	1⅛ tsp.	¾ tsp.
white wheat flour*	2¾ cup	2 cups	1⅓ cups
gluten flour	3 Tbsp.	2¼ Tbsp.	1½ Tbsp.
instant yeast	1¼ tsp.	¾ tsp.	⅔ tsp.

Add ingredients to bread maker in the order given. Select the proper setting and begin cycle.

It is easier to see the golden color of the eggs with white wheat flour. However, either white or red wheat will work.

Graham Bread

Graham flour, used to make graham crackers, is available in most grocery stores and in health food stores. It gives a delicious taste to whole wheat bread.

	LARGE	MEDIUM	SMALL
warm water	1½ cups	1⅛ cups	¾ cup
softened butter	1 Tbsp.	2 tsp.	1½ tsp.
honey	¼ cup	3 Tbsp.	2 Tbsp.
salt	1½ tsp.	1⅛ tsp.	¾ tsp.
graham flour	2 cups	1½ cups	1 cup
dry milk powder	¼ cup	3 Tbsp.	2 Tbsp.
wheat flour	1¼ cups	1 cup	⅔ cup
gluten flour	3 Tbsp.	2¼ Tbsp.	1½ Tbsp.
instant yeast	1¼ tsp.	1 tsp.	⅔ tsp.

Add all ingredients to the bread maker in the order given. Select the proper setting and begin the cycle.

Granola Bread

	LARGE	MEDIUM	SMALL
warm water	¾ cup	½ cup	¼ cup
buttermilk (scaled and cooled)	½ cup	⅜ cup	¼ cup
softened butter	2 Tbsp.	1½ Tbsp.	1 Tbsp.
honey	2 Tbsp.	1½ Tbsp.	1 Tbsp.
egg	1	1	1
sugar	2 Tbsp.	1½ Tbsp.	1 Tbsp.
salt	1½ tsp.	1 tsp.	¾ tsp.
granola (blended until fine)	1 cup	¾ cup	½ cup
wheat flour	2½ cups	1¾ cup	1¼ cup
gluten flour	3½ Tbsp.	2½ Tbsp.	1¾ Tbsp.
instant yeast	1½ tsp.	1⅛ tsp.	¾ tsp.

Add all the ingredients to the bread maker in the order given. Select the program and begin the cycle. If desired, 1 cup nuts can be added to the dough. Use the raisin bread setting and add the nuts when the machine beeps.

Hawaiian Coconut Bread

	LARGE	MEDIUM	SMALL
warm water	¼ cup	3 Tbsp.	2 Tbsp.
pineapple juice	½ cup	6 Tbsp.	¼ cup
crushed pineapple	½ cup	6 Tbsp.	¼ cup
shredded coconut	¾ cup	½ cup	¼ cup
butter	2 Tbsp.	1½ Tbsp.	1 Tbsp.
egg	1	1	1
sugar	1 Tbsp.	2 tsp.	1 tsp.
salt	1½ tsp.	1⅛ tsp.	¾ tsp.
wheat flour	2¾ cups	2 cups	1⅓ cups
gluten flour	3 Tbsp.	2¼ Tbsp.	1½ Tbsp.
instant yeast	1½ tsp.	1⅛ tsp.	¾ tsp.
macadamia nuts	¾ cup	½ cup	½ cup

Drain crushed pineapple, reserving liquid (use ½ cup in recipe). Add all the ingredients to the bread maker except the nuts. Select the raisin bread setting, and add the nuts when the machine beeps.

Healthy Caraway Seed Bread

	Large	**Medium**	**Small**
warm water	1 cup	¾ cup	½ cup
evaporated milk	⅓ cup	¼ cup	2½ Tbsp.
egg	1	1	1
honey	¼ cup	3 Tbsp.	2 Tbsp.
sugar	1 Tbsp.	2 tsp.	1½ tsp.
oil	1 Tbsp.	2 tsp.	1½ tsp.
caraway seeds	2 Tbsp.	1½ Tbsp.	1 Tbsp.
chopped nuts	¼ cup	3 Tbsp.	2 Tbsp.
corn flour (or meal)	½ cup	6 Tbsp.	¼ cup
rye flour	⅔ cup	½ cup	⅓ cup
wheat flour	2 cups	1½ cups	1 cup
gluten flour	4 Tbsp.	3 Tbsp.	2 Tbsp.
instant yeast	1½ tsp.	1⅛ tsp.	¾ tsp.

Measure ingredients into the bread maker in the order given. Select either the wheat or white bread setting, then begin the cycle.

Italian Bread

	LARGE	MEDIUM	SMALL
warm water	1½ cups	1⅛ cups	¾ cup
olive oil	1 Tbsp.	¾ Tbsp.	½ Tbsp.
Italian seasoning	1 tsp.	¾ tsp.	½ tsp.
garlic salt	1 tsp.	¾ tsp.	½ tsp.
Parmesan cheese	⅓ cup	¼ cup	2½ Tbsp.
sugar	1 Tbsp.	¾ Tbsp.	½ Tbsp.
wheat flour	3 cups	2¼ cups	1½ cups
gluten flour	3 Tbsp.	2¼ Tbsp.	1½ Tbsp.
instant yeast	1¼ tsp.	¾ tsp.	½ tsp.

Measure ingredients into the bread maker in the order given. Select the cycle desired, then begin the bread maker.

Lemon Poppy Seed Bread

	LARGE	MEDIUM	SMALL
lukewarm water	1⅓ cups	1 cup	⅔ cup
lemon juice	3 Tbsp.	2¼ Tbsp.	1½ Tbsp.
grated lemon peel	1 Tbsp.	2¼ Tbsp.	1½ Tbsp.
softened butter	2 Tbsp.	1½ Tbsp.	1 Tbsp.
salt	1½ tsp.	1⅛ tsp.	¾ tsp.
sugar	½ cup	6 Tbsp.	¼ cup
poppy seeds	1 Tbsp.	2 tsp.	1½ Tbsp.
wheat flour	3⅛ cups	2⅓ cups	1½ cups
gluten flour	3 Tbsp.	2¼ Tbsp.	1½ Tbsp.
instant yeast	1½ tsp.	1¼ tsp.	¾ tsp.
pecan halves	1 cup	¾ cup	½ cup

The delicate lemon flavor of this bread is more noticeable when using white wheat flour. If you use red wheat flour, you may increase the sugar by ½ and the lemon peel by ½. Measure all the ingredients into the bread maker in the order given. Program the machine for raisin bread. Add the pecans when the bread maker beeps.

Maple Oatmeal Bread

	LARGE	MEDIUM	SMALL
warm water	1⅓ cups	1 cup	⅔ cup
oil	1 Tbsp.	2 tsp.	1½ tsp.
maple syrup (real or imitation)	⅓ cup	3½ Tbsp.	2 Tbsp.
maple flavoring	1 tsp.	¾ tsp.	½ tsp.
salt	1½ tsp.	1⅛ tsp.	¾ tsp.
rolled oats	1 cup	¾ cup	½ cup
wheat flour	2¾ cups	2 cups	1⅓ cups
gluten flour	3 Tbsp.	2¼ Tbsp.	1½ Tbsp.
instant yeast	1½ tsp.	1⅛ tsp.	¾ tsp.

Rolled oats may be regular or quick. Place ingredients in bread maker in the order listed. Select the setting and begin the cycle.

Maple Pecan Bread

	LARGE	**MEDIUM**	**SMALL**
lukewarm water	1½ cups	1 cup	¾ cup
brown sugar	½ cup	6 Tbsp.	¼ cup
maple flavoring	1½ tsp.	1 tsp.	¾ tsp.
salt	1½ tsp.	1⅛ tsp.	¾ tsp.
softened butter	2 Tbsp.	1½ Tbsp.	1 Tbsp.
wheat flour	3⅛ cups	2¼ cups	1½ cups
gluten flour	3 Tbsp.	2¼ Tbsp.	1½ Tbsp.
instant yeast	1½ tsp.	1¼ tsp.	¾ tsp.
pecan or walnut halves	⅔ cup	½ cup	⅓ cup

Measure water, then other ingredients into bread maker, adding yeast last. Program the bread maker for raisin bread. When the machine beeps, add the nuts.

Mixed Vegetable Bread

	LARGE	MEDIUM	SMALL
warm water	1½ cups	1⅛ cups	¾ cup
salt	1½ tsp.	1⅛ tsp.	¾ tsp.
sugar	¼ cup	3 Tbsp.	2 Tbsp.
softened butter	2 Tbsp.	1½ Tbsp.	1 Tbsp.
wheat flour	3 cups	2¼ cups	1½ cups
dry milk powder	2 Tbsp.	1½ Tbsp.	1 Tbsp.
instant yeast	1½ tsp.	1⅛ tsp.	¾ tsp.
gluten flour	3 Tbsp.	2¼ Tbsp.	1½ Tbsp.
thawed and drained mixed vegetables	⅝ cup	½ cup	¼ cup

Add ingredients to bread maker in order given, saving out the mixed vegetables. Program the machine for raisin bread. When the machine beeps, add vegetables.

Oat Bread

	LARGE	MEDIUM	SMALL
warm water	1½ cups	1⅛ cups	¾ cup
lecithin	1½ tsp.	1⅛ tsp.	¾ tsp.
softened butter	1 Tbsp.	2 tsp.	1½ tsp.
salt	1½ tsp.	1⅛ tsp.	¾ tsp.
sugar	3 tsp.	2¼ tsp.	1½ tsp.
rolled oats	1 cup	¾ cup	½ cup
wheat flour	2½ cups	1¾ cups	1¼ cups
gluten flour	3 Tbsp.	2¼ Tbsp.	1½ Tbsp.
instant yeast	1¼ tsp.	1 tsp.	¾ tsp.

Blend rolled oats (regular or quick) in blender until fine. Add ingredients to the bread maker in the order given. Select the setting and start the cycle.

Oat Bran Apple Bread

	LARGE	MEDIUM	SMALL
warm apple juice	1½ cups	1⅛ cups	¾ cup
apples (peel/grate)	2 cups	1½ cups	1 cup
egg whites	2	1	1
honey	2 Tbsp.	1½ Tbsp.	1 Tbsp.
oil	1 Tbsp.	2 tsp.	1½ tsp.
cinnamon	1 tsp.	¾ tsp.	½ tsp.
salt	1½ tsp.	1⅛ tsp.	¾ tsp.
rolled oats	1 cup	¾ cup	½ cup
oat bran	2¼ cups	1¾ cups	1⅛ cups
wheat flour	3¼ cups	2½ cups	1¾ cups
gluten flour	4 Tbsp.	3 Tbsp.	2 Tbsp.
instant yeast	2 tsp.	1½ tsp.	1 tsp.

Measure ingredients into bread maker in order given. Use regular or instant rolled oats; do not blend them. The recipe is very large, and the pan will be quite full. The bread will not rise very much, but the finished loaf will be plenty tall. Select the wheat bread setting and begin the cycle.

Oat Bran Banana Bread

	LARGE	MEDIUM	SMALL
warm water	2⅛ cups	1½ cups	1 cup
sliced bananas	2	1 ½	1
egg whites	2	1	1
honey	2 Tbsp.	1½ Tbsp.	1 Tbsp.
oil	2 Tbsp.	1½ Tbsp.	1 Tbsp.
salt	1½ tsp.	1⅛ tsp.	¾ tsp.
oat bran	2¼ cups	1¾ cups	1⅛ cups
rolled oats	1 cup	¾ cup	½ cup
wheat flour	3 cups	2¼ cups	1½ cups
gluten flour	4 Tbsp.	3 Tbsp.	2 Tbsp.
instant yeast	2 tsp.	1½ tsp.	1 tsp.

Measure ingredients into bread maker in order given. This recipe is large, and the pan will be more full than usual. The bread will only rise to the top of the pan. Select the cycle, then start the bread maker.

Oat Bran Bread

	LARGE	MEDIUM	SMALL
lukewarm water	1½ cups	1⅛ cups	¾ cup
molasses	2 Tbsp.	1½ Tbsp.	1 Tbsp.
oat bran	½ cup	6 Tbsp.	¼ cup
honey	1 Tbsp.	2 tsp.	1½ tsp.
lecithin	1½ tsp.	1 tsp.	¾ tsp.
oil	1 tsp.	¾ tsp.	½ tsp.
salt	1½ tsp.	1⅛ tsp.	¾ tsp.
wheat flour	3¼ cups	2½ cups	1¾ cups
gluten flour	3 Tbsp.	2¼ Tbsp.	1½ Tbsp.
instant yeast	1¼ tsp.	1 tsp.	¾ tsp.

Measure ingredients in order given. Select bread making cycle, then start the bread maker.

Onion Dill Bread

	LARGE	MEDIUM	SMALL
lukewarm water	1½ cups	1 cup	⅔ cup
sugar	4 Tbsp.	3 Tbsp.	2 Tbsp.
dried onion *or*	2 Tbsp.	1½ Tbsp.	1 Tbsp.
chopped onion	½ cup	⅓ cup	¼ cup
salt	1½ tsp.	1 tsp.	¾ tsp.
egg	1	1	1
softened butter	1 Tbsp.	2 tsp.	1½ tsp.
dill seeds	4 tsp.	3 tsp.	2 tsp.
poppy seeds	1½ tsp.	1 tsp.	¾ tsp.
wheat flour	3 cups	2¼ cups	1½ cups
instant dry milk	½ cup	⅓ cup	¼ cup
gluten flour	3 Tbsp.	2¼ Tbsp.	1½ Tbsp.
instant yeast	1¼ tsp.	1 tsp.	⅔ tsp.

Measure ingredients into the bread maker in the order given. Program the bread maker, then begin the cycle.

Onion Soup Bread

	LARGE	MEDIUM	SMALL
lukewarm water	¼ cup	3 Tbsp.	2 Tbsp.
oil	1½ Tbsp.	1 Tbsp.	2 tsp.
egg	1	1	1
cottage cheese	¾ cup	½ cup	⅜ cup
sour cream	¾ cup	½ cup	⅜ cup
sugar	3 Tbsp.	2 Tbsp.	1½ Tbsp.
wheat flour	3¼ cups	2½ cups	1¾ cups
baking soda	½ tsp.	¼ tsp.	¼ tsp.
Lipton's™ Onion Soup Mix (dry)	¾ envelope	½ envelope	⅜ envelope
gluten flour	3 Tbsp.	2¼ Tbsp.	1½ Tbsp.
instant yeast	1½ tsp.	1 tsp.	¾ tsp.

Measure water, oil, and egg in to the bread maker. Slightly warm the cottage cheese and sour cream, then add them to the bread maker. Add the remaining ingredients in the order given. Select the wheat bread cycle, then start the machine.

Orange Bread

This bread is very good when sliced bread is spread with a mixture of equal parts cream cheese and honey.

	LARGE	MEDIUM	SMALL
lukewarm water	⅓ cup	3½ Tbsp.	2 ½ Tbsp.
orange juice (warmed)	1⅓ cups	1 cup	⅔ cup
sugar	¼ cup	3 Tbsp.	2 Tbsp.
salt	1½ tsp.	1 tsp.	¾ tsp.
lecithin	2 tsp.	1½ tsp.	1 tsp.
softened butter	2 Tbsp.	1½ Tbsp.	1 Tbsp.
grated orange peel	2 Tbsp.	1½ Tbsp.	1 Tbsp.
white wheat flour	3½ cups	2½ cups	1¾ cups
gluten flour	3 Tbsp.	2¼ Tbsp.	1½ Tbsp.
instant yeast	1¼ tsp.	1 tsp.	¾ tsp.

Measure ingredients into the bread maker in the order given. Program the machine and start the cycle.

Peanut Bread

	LARGE	MEDIUM	SMALL
warm water	1¼ cups	¾ cup	½ cup
egg	1	1	1
oil	2 Tbsp.	1½ Tbsp.	1 Tbsp.
sugar	3 Tbsp.	2¼ Tbsp.	1½ Tbsp.
salt	¾ tsp.	½ tsp.	¼ tsp.
wheat flour	2¾ cups	2 cups	1⅔ cups
salted peanuts	¾ cup	½ cup	⅜ cup
gluten flour	3 Tbsp.	2¼ Tbsp.	1½ Tbsp.
instant yeast	1½ tsp.	1 tsp.	¾ tsp.

Add ingredients in order given. Set the bread maker on the raisin bread cycle. Add the peanuts when the machine beeps.

Peanut Butter Bread

	LARGE	**MEDIUM**	**SMALL**
lukewarm water	1½ cups	1⅛ cups	¾ cup
salt	1½ tsp.	1 tsp.	¾ tsp.
brown sugar	½ cup	⅓ cup	¼ cup
peanut butter (creamy or chunky)	¾ cup	½ cup	⅜ cup
wheat flour	3¼ cups	2½ cups	1⅔ cups
gluten flour	3 Tbsp.	2¼ Tbsp.	1½ Tbsp.
instant yeast	1½ tsp.	1 tsp.	¾ tsp.

Add ingredients to bread maker in order given. Make sure peanut butter is at room temperature. Select the cycle, and start the bread maker.

Pecan Date Bread

	LARGE	MEDIUM	SMALL
lukewarm water	1½ cups	1 cup	¾ cup
softened butter	2 Tbsp.	1½ Tbsp.	1 Tbsp.
salt	1½ tsp.	1⅛ tsp.	¾ tsp.
honey	2 Tbsp.	1½ Tbsp.	1 Tbsp.
wheat flour	3¼ cups	2½ cups	1⅔ cups
gluten flour	3 Tbsp.	2¼ Tbsp.	1½ Tbsp.
instant yeast	1½ tsp.	1 tsp.	¾ tsp.
chopped dates	½ cup	⅜ cup	¼ cup
pecan halves	½ cup	⅜ cup	¼ cup

Measure first seven ingredients into the bread maker. Select the raisin bread cycle. Start the machine. When the bread maker beeps, add the dates and pecans.

Pecan Onion Bread

	LARGE	MEDIUM	SMALL
scalded warm milk	1⅛ cups	¾ cup	½ cup
softened butter	¼ cup	3 Tbsp.	2 Tbsp.
sugar	1½ tsp.	1 tsp.	¾ tsp.
salt	1½ tsp.	1 tsp.	¾ tsp.
chopped red onion	½ cup	⅜ cup	¼ cup
wheat flour	3 cups	2¼ cups	1½ cups
gluten flour	3 Tbsp.	2¼ Tbsp.	1½ Tbsp.
instant yeast	1½ tsp.	1 tsp.	¾ tsp.
pecans (chopped or halved)	¾ cup	½ cup	⅜ cup

Measure ingredients into bread maker in the order listed, except the pecans. Set the machine on the raisin bread cycle. When the bread maker beeps, add the pecans.

Pepper Spice Bread

This bread is rich and spicy. It is a delicious complement to any mild soup or stew.

	LARGE	MEDIUM	SMALL
warm water	1 cup	¾ cup	½ cup
corn syrup	2 Tbsp.	1½ Tbsp.	1 Tbsp.
honey	2 Tbsp.	1½ Tbsp.	1 Tbsp.
egg	1	1	1
chopped pecans	¼ cup	3 Tbsp.	2 Tbsp.
softened butter	¼ cup	3 Tbsp.	2 Tbsp.
sugar	¼ cup	3 Tbsp.	2 Tbsp.
salt	1 tsp.	¾ tsp.	½ tsp.
black pepper	½ tsp.	¼ tsp.	¼ tsp.
anise seed	1 tsp.	¾ tsp.	½ tsp.
cinnamon	¼ tsp.	¼ tsp.	⅛ tsp.
allspice	¼ tsp.	¼ tsp.	⅛ tsp.
wheat flour	3 cups	2¼ cups	1½ cups
gluten flour	3 Tbsp.	2¼ Tbsp.	1½ Tbsp.
instant yeast	1½ tsp.	1⅛ tsp.	¾ tsp.

Measure ingredients into bread maker in the order given. Select the wheat bread option, then start the machine.

Prune Bread

	LARGE	MEDIUM	SMALL
warm water	1¼ cups	1 cup	¾ cup
pitted prunes (quartered)	1 cup	¾ cup	½ cup
butter	1 Tbsp.	2 tsp.	1½ tsp.
brown sugar	3 Tbsp.	2¼ Tbsp.	1½ Tbsp.
salt	1½ tsp.	1 tsp.	¾ tsp.
wheat flour	3 cups	2¼ cups	1½ cups
gluten flour	3 Tbsp.	2¼ Tbsp.	1½ Tbsp.
instant yeast	1½ tsp.	1 tsp.	¾ tsp.

Measure ingredients into the bread maker in the order given. Select the cycle, then start the machine.

Pumpernickel Bread

It has a superb flavor!

	LARGE	MEDIUM	SMALL
warm water	1¼ cups	1 cup	¾ cup
oil	1 Tbsp.	2 tsp.	1½ tsp.
molasses	3 Tbsp.	2¼ Tbsp.	1½ Tbsp.
cocoa	1 Tbsp.	2 tsp.	1½ tsp.
salt	1½ tsp.	1⅛ tsp.	¾ tsp.
caraway seed	2 tsp.	1½ tsp.	1 tsp.
wheat flour	2¾ cups	2 cups	1⅓ cups
rye flour	½ cup	⅜ cup	¼ cup
gluten flour	4 Tbsp.	3 Tbsp.	2 Tbsp.
instant yeast	1½ tsp.	1 tsp.	¾ tsp.

Measure ingredients into bread maker in the order given. Select the cycle, then start the machine. Use the light crust setting if your machine has one, as this bread will be very dark.

Pumpkin Bread

This bread is very good as toast for breakfast.

	LARGE	MEDIUM	SMALL
lukewarm water	1⅓ cups	1 cup	⅔ cup
pumpkin	⅔ cup	½ cup	⅓ cup
oil	2 Tbsp.	1½ Tbsp.	1 Tbsp.
brown sugar	⅓ cup	3 Tbsp.	2 Tbsp.
salt	1½ tsp.	1 tsp.	¾ tsp.
cinnamon	1½ tsp.	1 tsp.	¾ tsp.
cloves	½ tsp.	⅓ tsp.	¼ tsp.
nutmeg	½ tsp.	⅓ tsp.	¼ tsp.
ginger	½ tsp.	⅓ tsp.	¼ tsp.
wheat flour	3½ cups	2¾ cups	1¾ cups
gluten flour	3 Tbsp.	2¼ Tbsp.	1½ Tbsp.
instant yeast	1½ tsp.	1 tsp.	¾ tsp.

Measure all the ingredients into bread maker in the order given. Program the bread maker, then begin the cycle. Since the pumpkin, spices, and wheat flour create very dark bread, be sure to use the light crust setting.

Raisin Bran Bread

	LARGE	MEDIUM	SMALL
warm water	1 cup	¾ cup	½ cup
lecithin	1½ tsp.	1 tsp.	¾ tsp.
oil	1 tsp.	¾ tsp.	½ tsp.
brown sugar	¼ cup	3 Tbsp.	2 Tbsp.
salt	1 tsp.	¾ tsp.	½ tsp.
wheat flour	1¾ cups	1⅓ cups	¾ cup
raisin bran cereal	1½ cups	1⅛ cups	¾ cup
baking soda	¼ tsp.	⅛ tsp.	⅛ tsp.
gluten flour	3 Tbsp.	2¼ Tbsp.	1½ Tbsp.
instant yeast	1¼ tsp.	1 tsp.	¾ tsp.

Measure all ingredients into bread maker in the order listed. Select the cycle, then start the machine. This bread may not rise very high, but it is a very nutritious and tasty bread.

Raisin Cinnamon Bread

	LARGE	MEDIUM	SMALL
lukewarm water	1⅓ cups	1 cup	⅔ cup
sugar	½ cup	⅓ cup	¼ cup
salt	1½ tsp.	1 tsp.	¾ tsp.
butter	2 Tbsp.	1½ Tbsp.	1 Tbsp.
wheat flour	2¾ cups	2¼ cups	1⅓ cups
cinnamon	1½ tsp.	1 tsp.	¾ tsp.
instant dry milk	½ cup	⅓ cup	¼ cup
gluten flour	3 Tbsp.	2 Tbsp.	1½ Tbsp.
instant yeast	1½ tsp.	1 tsp.	¾ tsp.
raisins	1 cup	¾ cup	½ cup
nuts	½ cup	⅓ cup	¼ cup

Measure warm water into the bread maker, followed by the other ingredients. Add gluten flour and yeast last. Program your bread maker for raisin bread. After dough is mixed together, make sure that the dough is the desired consistency, adding a little more flour or water as needed. When the machine beeps, add raisins and nuts.

Six-grain Bread

	LARGE	MEDIUM	SMALL
lukewarm water	1½ cups	1 cups	¾ cup
lecithin	2 Tbsp.	1½ Tbsp.	1 Tbsp.
salt	1½ tsp.	1 tsp.	¾ tsp.
honey or molasses	2 Tbsp.	1½ Tbsp.	1 Tbsp.
wheat flour	3 cups	2¼ cups	1½ cups
six-grain cereal	¼ cup	3 Tbsp.	2 Tbsp.
gluten flour	3 Tbsp.	2¼ Tbsp.	1½ Tbsp.
instant yeast	1¼ tsp.	1 tsp.	¾ tsp.

Measure water into bread maker. Add rest of ingredients in the order given. Program the bread maker and start the machine.

South of the Border Bread

	Large	Medium	Small
warm water	1¼ cups	1 cup	¾ cup
egg	1	1	1
sugar	1 Tbsp.	2 tsp.	1½ tsp.
lecithin	1 Tbsp.	2 tsp.	1½ tsp.
salt	1 tsp.	¾ tsp.	½ tsp.
shredded cheese	½ cup	6 Tbsp.	¼ cup
diced chilies	1 Tbsp.	2 tsp.	1½ tsp.
corn (drained)	½ cup	⅜ cup	¼ cup
wheat flour	2¾ cups	2 cups	1⅓ cups
cornmeal	¾ cup	½ cup	¼ cup
gluten flour	3 Tbsp.	2¼ Tbsp.	1½ Tbsp.
instant yeast	1¾ tsp.	1¼ tsp.	1 tsp.

Add ingredients to the bread maker in the order given. Select the desired setting, then start the machine.

Tomato Bread

	LARGE	MEDIUM	SMALL
warm water plus 1 egg to equal	1½ cups	1 cup	¾ cup
sugar	4 Tbsp.	3 Tbsp.	2 Tbsp.
lecithin	1 tsp.	¾ tsp.	½ tsp.
oil	2 tsp.	1½ tsp.	1 tsp.
salt	1½ tsp.	1 tsp.	¾ tsp.
dried tomato (blended)	½ cup	⅓ cup	¼ cup
wheat flour	3 cups	2¼ cups	1½ cups
gluten flour	3 Tbsp.	2¼ Tbsp.	1½ Tbsp.
instant yeast	1½ tsp.	1 tsp.	¾ tsp.
pecans	1 cup	¾ cup	½ cup
macadamia nuts	¾ cup	½ cup	⅓ cup

Measure ingredients into bread maker in the order given, except the nuts. Select the raisin bread cycle. Add the nuts when the machine beeps.

CHAPTER 4
Causes of Poor-quality Bread

Sometimes you may not be pleased with your bread, or you may have noticed a particular problem with your bread. If so, you may be able to find a quick and easy solution in this chapter.

The problems and solutions in the first section relate to making bread by hand or by a bread mixer, where the bread has to bake in an oven.

The second section refers to difficulties that are specific to automatic bread makers.

An asterisk (*) will mark problems and solutions that are common to bread made by any of these methods.

HANDMADE AND BREADMIXER BREAD

- **Does your finished bread have a poor shape?**
  » You may have left some air bubbles in your dough before the last rise in the pan. Also, there may have been uneven heat distribution in the oven. Make sure that your loaves have enough space between them while baking for the air and heat to circulate evenly between the loaves.

- **Is your bread crumbly, with poor volume?***
  » Your flour may have been too coarsely milled, the wheat could have been poor bread making quality, or the dough may not have been kneaded

long enough. Any of these factors would have kept the gluten from developing enough to bind the bread together. The result is crumbly bread.

» If too much oil or fat is added, it can over-tenderize the dough as well. The bread may have been baked before it had risen sufficiently, or the oven temperature may have been too low. In an oven that is too cool, the loaves will not set quickly enough. They continue to rise until the cell walls collapse.

» When the bread finally bakes, the loaves are flat and crumbly. If the bread is not crumbly, but the volume is poor, your yeast may be old or ineffective. Try using new yeast, making sure that the water temperature and the other ingredients are not too hot or cold.

• **Does your bread hang over the side of the pan on one or both sides?**

» Your dough may have been too soft. Use a little more flour next time. Also, if the wheat or flour is poor in bread making quality, the dough cannot sustain itself. Try different wheat or flour. The dough may have been allowed to rise too long (more than doubled in size), or there may have been too much dough in the pan to begin with.

» Finally, if the oven was too cool, or if the heat was not able to distribute evenly (if your pans were too close together in the oven), the bread may have fallen over the side of the pan where the heat was the lowest.

• **Is there a crack along one or both sides of your loaf after baking?**

» Uneven heat circulation in the oven could have caused the cracks. Make sure that the pans are far enough apart to allow heat and air circulation while the bread is baking. Dough that is too dry can also crack during baking. Use a little less flour next time.

• **Are there air bubbles under the top crust after baking?**

» Mold your loaves in such a way that the air bubbles are worked out before the loaves are placed in the pans. Also, be sure that your bread doesn't rise too high before baking. Finally, the oven has to be hot enough to set the yeast cells in the dough immediately, or the bread will rise too high in the oven before it bakes, creating an air bubble under the crust.

- **Do deep cracks appear in the sides or top of your loaves after baking?**
  » Usually, deep cracks are caused by dough that has not been kneaded long enough, and the gluten has not developed. The bread just won't hold together and it cracks as it bakes. It might also be a good idea to try a different flour or wheat.

- **Does your bread have an abnormally thick crust that is hard to chew?**
  » You may not have kneaded the bread long enough. The gluten won't hold the bread together, making the finished product heavy and crusty. If the rising period was too long, the dough may have collapsed, also causing a thick, heavy loaf and crust.
  » An oven that was too cool would have the same effect; it would allow the bread to continue rising in the oven until it collapsed. The loaf would be heavy and the crust would be thick.

The addition of a little lecithin may tenderize the dough and the crust. Use lecithin in place of half of the oil or butter in the recipe. If the bread burns in the oven, the crust will be too hard. Covering the loaf with aluminum foil the last 10–15 minutes in the oven can prevent excess oven browning.

- **Are the cell walls inside your sliced bread big and thick instead of small and delicate?**
  » If your flour has not been milled fine enough, the bread will be coarse and heavy.
  » If the dough has not been kneaded enough, the gluten will not develop properly, and again, the cell walls will be thick and large.
  » If the dough has not been allowed to rise enough, the cell walls inside the bread will be compact, and will appear thick and heavy.
  » The bread making quality of the wheat or flour can make a difference as well. Try a different wheat or flour, and make sure to use 3 tablespoons of gluten flour per loaf of bread. Sometimes we are using wheat or flour that just does not develop gluten sufficiently.

- **Are there streaks in your finished loaves?**
  - » Streaks are caused by adding flour after the kneading process has been completed. The flour isn't able to incorporate into the dough sufficiently, so it forms streaks. Oil or fat on your hands while you mold dough into loaves can also cause streaks. Use a little less oil. Streaks won't generally hurt the quality of the bread.
- **Are your loaves dense and thick at the bottom, but crumbly at the top?**
  - » If loaves are placed on a surface that is too cool during rising, it will prevent the loaf from rising uniformly. The top of the loaf will rise, but the bottom will stay compact. If your oven is too cool during baking, the loaves will continue to rise too long in the oven before the outside crust becomes hard enough to prevent any more rising. If you do not use enough dough in your pans, then allow it to rise too high, the resulting loaf will be crumbly at the top as well.
- **Are your loaves coarse in texture?***
  - » Poorly milled wheat, as well as insufficient kneading will prevent the proper development of gluten. The texture of your finished bread will be coarse and heavy.
  - » If dough is not allowed to rise long enough, or if it is too cool to rise, it will be compact and coarse.
  - » If the yeast is old, or if salt has come in contact too intensely with the yeast, the yeast may not perform well enough. The bread will not rise sufficiently, and will actually have a good texture, but you will not be able to appreciate the finished product because it will be heavy and compact.

AUTOMATIC BREAD MAKER BREAD

- **Is your loaf compact and heavy without enough loft?**
  - » Your yeast may be old. New yeast may make a difference. Your flour may not be sufficient in its bread making quality. You can either try different wheat or flour, or you can keep using the same flour and increase your gluten flour by 25 percent.
  - » Your wheat may be milled too coarsely, preventing gluten from developing.

» You may have added too much flour, making the dough too heavy. Finally, your bread maker may not have enough rising time for wheat bread. You can always try adding 25 percent more instant yeast to your recipe.

- **Does your loaf rise and then collapse before baking?**

  » There may be too much liquid in the recipe. Add a little more flour next time.

  » The rise time may be too long. It may help to cut down the amount of yeast in the recipe by about 25 percent.

  » The recipe may be too small for the pan.

  » The ingredients may be too warm, and the dough will rise too quickly.

- **Does your loaf rise so high that it is crumbly at the top?**

  » If the dough is too soft, it will rise too quickly. Add more flour next time.

  » If you have cut down on the salt in your recipe, the yeast will not be controlled as well, and may cause the dough to rise too high.

  » Also, if there is too much yeast in the dough, the bread rises too quickly and too high. You can try using 25 percent less yeast.

  » Finally, the recipe may be too large for the bread maker. Making a smaller recipe may help.

- **Does your bread taste yeasty?**

  » Use less yeast, less sugar, or both.

- **Is the top of your loaf bulgy and cracked?**

  » The dough is too dry and doesn't form well. Use less flour, or try different flour next time.

CHAPTER 5

Whole Wheat Muffins

Whole wheat bread making can be such a challenge, but it can be so rewarding. While learning to master the principles of bread making, you are also learning to use whole wheat flour. Since whole wheat flour is so nutritious, it can be rewarding to also use it in other baked goods.

Whole wheat muffins are easy to make and take much less time than yeast bread. They are good for breakfast, after-school snacks, or even the foundation of a quick lunch. If desired, substitute applesauce for the oil in any of these recipes to reduce fat content.

In making whole wheat muffins, one does not need to be so concerned about the bread making quality of the wheat. Muffins do not need a strong protein foundation in the dough because they are held together by liquid, fats, and eggs. Yeast is not used for leavening, but fast acting baking powder and/or baking soda are used.

If you have wheat or wheat flour that does not make particularly good bread, it will probably make fabulous muffins. Either hard white or hard red wheat flour can be used.

If a muffin recipe calls for mild flavoring ingredients (like lemon poppy seed muffins), the white wheat flour will probably be better, because the mild flavor will not overpower the other ingredients. That is really the only consideration when choosing whether to use white wheat flour or red wheat flour.

Carrot Whole Grain Muffins (makes 12)

1 cup rolled oats
1 tsp. cinnamon
½ cup whole wheat flour
½ cup water
½ cup corn meal
¼ cup oil

¼ cup brown sugar
2 eggs
2½ tsp. baking powder
1¼ cup shredded carrots
½ tsp. salt (firmly packed)

Preheat oven to 400 degrees. Stir dry ingredients together. Mix water, oil, and eggs together. Stir slightly, and then add carrots. Add 2nd mixture to the dry ingredients. Stir until moistened. If desired, add ½ cup chopped nuts. Fill sprayed muffin cups ⅔ full. Bake 20–25 minutes.

Cheesecake Muffins (makes 16)

MUFFINS:

½ cup chocolate chips
⅓ cup soft butter
1 egg
1½ cups white wheat flour
1 tsp. vanilla
1 tsp. baking soda
1 cup water
½ tsp. salt
½ cup sugar

FILLING:

8 oz. softened cream cheese
⅓ cup sugar
1 egg
pinch of salt
½ cup chocolate chips

Filling: Combine cream cheese, sugar, egg, and salt. Beat until creamy. Stir in ½ cup chocolate chips. Set aside.

Muffins: Preheat oven to 350 degrees. Melt over hot water (not boiling) remaining ½ cup chocolate chips. Stir until smooth. Remove from heat and set aside. In small bowl, combine sugar, butter, egg, and vanilla. Beat well. Add melted chips. Beat in flour alternately with water. Spoon half of batter into 16 sprayed muffin cups. Spoon 1 slightly rounded tablespoon filling over batter. Spoon remaining batter over filling. Bake 25 minutes. Sprinkle with powdered sugar.

Chocolate Breakfast Muffins (makes 12)

1¾ cups white wheat flour
1 beaten egg
1 cup sugar
⅓ cup softened butter
3 tsp. baking powder
½ cup chopped nuts

¾ tsp. salt
1 cup milk
5 Tbsp. cocoa powder
1 tsp. vanilla
1 cup chocolate chips (opt.)

Preheat oven to 400 degrees. Cream butter and 1 cup sugar together. Add egg and vanilla; mix well. Mix flour, baking powder, salt, cocoa powder, nuts, and chocolate chips together. Add flour mixture alternately with milk to creamed butter mixture. Fill sprayed muffin cups ⅔ full. Bake 25 minutes.

Chocolate Chip Muffins (makes 12–14)

2¼ cups white wheat flour
3 eggs
3 tsp. baking powder
¾ cup butter
½ tsp. salt

1 cup chocolate chips
1½ cups sugar
1 cup water
½ cup cocoa
1 tsp. vanilla

Preheat oven to 375 degrees. Cream butter and sugar. Add eggs, then cocoa. Add salt, baking powder, and vanilla. Mix well. Add flour alternately with water. Mix until moistened, then add chocolate chips. Add a little more water if batter is too stiff. Spoon into sprayed muffin cups. Bake 20–22 minutes.

If you want to make the larger size muffins, double the recipe. Bake 25–28 minutes.

Lemon Tea Muffins (makes 18)

1 cup white wheat flour
2 eggs (separated)
1½ tsp. baking powder
3 Tbsp. lemon juice
¼ tsp. salt
1 tsp. grated lemon peel

½ cup butter
½ cup powdered sugar
½ cup sugar
1½ Tbsp. lemon juice
2½ tsp. poppy seeds

Preheat oven to 375 degrees. Mix together flour, baking powder, salt, and poppy seeds. Cream butter and ½ cup sugar. Beat egg yolks; blend well with creamed mixture. Add flour mixture alternately with lemon juice. Do not over mix. Beat egg whites until stiff. Fold whites and lemon peel into the batter. Fill sprayed muffin cups ⅔ full. Bake 15–20 minutes.

After removing from oven, combine ½ cup powdered sugar and 1½ tablespoons lemon juice. Drizzle over muffins while hot.

Maple Bran Muffins (makes 12)

¾ cup wheat bran
½ cup milk
1¼ cups whole wheat flour
1 beaten egg
3 tsp. baking powder

¼ cup oil or applesauce
½ tsp. salt
½ cup maple syrup
½ cup chopped nuts

Preheat oven to 400 degrees. Combine dry ingredients, including chopped nuts. Mix milk, egg, oil or applesauce, and maple syrup together; blend into dry ingredients, stirring just until moistened. Spoon into sprayed muffin cups. Bake for 18–20 minutes.

Glaze: Combine ½ cup powdered sugar with 1 tablespoon maple syrup. Spread over warm muffins.

Oat Bran Muffins (makes 12)

1½ cups oat bran
1 egg
½ cup wheat flour
2 Tbsp. applesauce or oil
3 Tbsp. brown sugar
½ cup apple juice
2 tsp. baking powder

2 Tbsp. honey
½ tsp. salt
1 cup grated apple
1 tsp. cinnamon
2 Tbsp. raisins or nuts
¼ cup skim milk

Preheat oven to 400 degrees. Mix together dry ingredients. Mix egg, applesauce or oil, apple juice, honey, apple, and raisins or nuts. Pour all at once into dry ingredients. Mix gently until moistened. Spoon into muffin papers or sprayed muffin cups. Bake 20 minutes.

Oat Bran Banana Muffins (makes 12)

2¼ cups oat bran
1¼ cups skim milk
1 Tbsp. baking powder
2 ripe bananas, mashed

¼ cup brown sugar
2 egg whites
½ tsp. salt
2 Tbsp. vegetable oil or applesauce

Preheat oven to 425 degrees. Mix dry ingredients (including nuts) in a large bowl. Mix milk, bananas, egg whites, and oil or applesauce together. Add dry ingredients and mix lightly. Bake 17 minutes in sprayed muffin cups.

Oatmeal Muffins (makes 12)

1 cup rolled oats
1 cup water
1 cup whole wheat flour
1 egg
½ cup sugar

¼ cup oil or applesauce
1 Tbsp. baking powder
⅓ cup dry milk powder
½ cup chopped nuts (opt.)

Preheat oven to 400 degrees. Combine all dry ingredients and the nuts together. Combine water, egg, and oil or applesauce. Stir wet mixture gently into dry ingredients until moistened. Fill sprayed muffin cups ⅔ full. Bake 20–25 minutes.

Peanut Butter Muffins (makes 18)

2 cups whole wheat flour
2 Tbsp. butter
½ cup sugar
1 cup milk
3 tsp. baking powder

2 beaten eggs
½ tsp. salt
½ cup chunky or creamy peanut butter
½ cup chopped peanuts
½ cup melted jelly

Preheat oven to 400 degrees. Sift together flour, sugar, baking powder, and salt. Cut in peanut butter and butter until mixture resembles coarse crumbs. Add milk and eggs all at once, stirring just until moistened. Fill sprayed muffin cups ⅔ full. Bake 15–17 minutes. Brush tops with melted jelly and dip in peanuts.

Pralines and Cream Muffins (makes 12)

½ cup brown sugar
1 cup rolled oats (regular or quick)
⅓ cup softened butter
3 oz. softened cream cheese
1 Tbsp. baking powder
⅔ cup milk

½ tsp. salt
1 egg
¾ cup chopped pecans, divided
1 tsp. maple flavoring
¾ cup white wheat flour

Preheat oven to 400 degrees. In medium bowl, beat brown sugar, butter, and cream cheese until smooth. Add milk, egg, and maple flavoring. Mix well. Add combined dry ingredients and ½ cup pecans, stirring only until moistened. Fill sprayed muffin cups ¾ full. Sprinkle with remaining ¼ cup pecans. Bake 20–22 minutes.

Pumpkin Muffins (makes 12)

1½ cups whole wheat flour
1 beaten egg
½ cup sugar
½ cup milk
2½ tsp. baking powder
½ cup mashed pumpkin
½ tsp. salt

½ cup raisins (opt.)
½ tsp. cinnamon
½ tsp. nutmeg
2 Tbsp. oil
½ cup chopped nuts (opt.)
1 cup chocolate chips (opt.)

Preheat oven to 400 degrees. Mix dry ingredients together, including the nuts, raisins, and/or chocolate chips. Then stir in liquid ingredients all at once. Mix until moistened. Fill sprayed muffin cups ⅔ full. Bake 18–20 minutes.

Streusel-filled Muffins (makes 12)

MUFFINS:

1½ cups white wheat flour
¼ cup softened butter
½ cup sugar
1 beaten egg
2½ tsp. baking powder
½ cup water
½ tsp. salt
¼ cup dry powdered milk

FILLING:

¼ cup brown sugar
1 tsp. cinnamon
¼ cup chopped nuts
1 Tbsp. butter
1 Tbsp. flour

Preheat oven to 350 degrees. Measure flour, sugar, baking powder, and salt into mixing bowl. Cut in ¼ cup butter until mixture resembles cornmeal. Mix egg and water; add all at once to dry ingredients. Stir just until moistened.

For filling, combine brown sugar, nuts, 1 tablespoon flour, cinnamon, and butter. Place half the muffin batter in sprayed muffin cups. Measure about 1½ teaspoon of filling mixture and sprinkle on each muffin. Top with remaining batter. Bake 20 minutes. Makes 12.

Wheat Bran Banana Muffins (makes 10)

1 cup whole wheat flour
1 egg, beaten
3 Tbsp. sugar
1 cup mashed banana
2½ tsp. baking powder

¼ cup milk
½ tsp. salt
2 Tbsp. oil (or applesauce)
1 cup wheat bran

Preheat oven to 400 degrees. Sift together flour, sugar, baking powder, and salt. Stir in bran. Mix remaining ingredients. Add all at once to flour mixture, stirring to moisten. Fill sprayed muffin cups. Bake 20–25 minutes.

Wheat Bran Muffins (makes 12)

1 cup wheat bran
2 Tbsp. oil (or applesauce)
1 cup whole wheat flour
1 egg
½ tsp. salt
2½ tsp. baking powder

½ cup chopped nuts
⅓ cup sugar
¾ cup water (more if batter is dry)
¼ cup dry powdered milk
½ cup raisins (opt.)

Preheat oven to 400 degrees. Mix dry ingredients together. Add oil, egg, raisins (opt.), nuts, and ¾ cup water. Fill sprayed muffin cups ⅔ full. Bake 15–20 minutes.

Whole Wheat Breakfast Muffins (makes 12)

1¾ cups whole wheat flour
1 beaten egg
½ cup sugar
¾ cup milk
3 tsp. baking powder

⅓ cup oil
¾ tsp. salt
½ cup chopped nuts or
1 cup well-drained blueberries

Preheat oven to 400 degrees. Sift dry ingredients into bowl; make a well in the center. Combine egg, milk, and oil. Add all at once to dry ingredients along with nuts or blueberries. Gently fold ingredients together, just until moistened. Fill sprayed muffin cups ⅔ full. Bake about 25 minutes.

Quick Mix for Muffins, Pancakes, Breads, and Cakes

A whole wheat quick mix can speed up your time in the kitchen while you are learning to cook with all that whole wheat flour in your pantry. As was stated earlier, either white wheat flour or red wheat flour will work equally well. Sometimes the white wheat flour is more desirable because of its milder flavor.

1 cup whole wheat flour
½ cup sugar
2½ tsp. baking powder
¾ tsp. salt
½ cup instant or non-instant powdered milk
¼ cup powdered eggs

Add 1 cup of any of the following: corn meal, wheat bran, oat bran, rolled oats, or ¾ cup additional wheat flour. If using powdered eggs, add 1½ cups water and mix well. If using fresh eggs, use one egg and 1½ cups water to mixed dry ingredients. Spoon batter into sprayed muffin cups. Bake at 375 degrees for 20 minutes. Makes 12.

To make large quantities of this mix, combine the following and store in air-tight container. It is best stored in the refrigerator. That way, it should last for 3 months.

8 cups whole wheat flour
3½ cups sugar
½ cup baking powder
2 Tbsp. salt
4 cups instant or non-instant powdered milk
2 cups powdered eggs

Banana Nut Muffins (makes 12–15)

- 1¾ cups of quick mix
- ¾ cup wheat flour
- 1 tsp. baking powder
- 1 cup mashed banana
- 2 Tbsp. applesauce
- ½ cup water
- ½ cup chopped nuts (opt.)

Mix well, then spoon into sprayed muffin cups. Bake in preheated 400 degree oven for 20–25 minutes.

Blueberry Muffins (makes 12–15)

- 1¾ cups quick mix
- ¾ cup wheat flour
- ¼ cup sugar
- 1½ cups water
- 1 cup frozen or fresh blueberries.

Mix well. Spoon into sprayed muffin cups. Bake at 400 degrees for 20 minutes.

Bran Muffins (makes 12)

1¾ cups quick mix
1 cup wheat bran or oat bran
1½ cups water
2 Tbsp. oil

Stir gently, then spoon batter into sprayed muffin cups. Bake at 375 degrees for 20–25 minutes.

Cheesecake Muffins (makes 12)

1¾ cups quick mix
4 Tbsp. brown sugar
¾ cup wheat flour
6 oz. softened cream cheese
1 tsp. maple flavoring
1 cup water
½ cup chopped pecans (opt.)

Mix dry ingredients, then gently add cream cheese. Stir in maple flavoring, water, and pecans. Spoon into sprayed muffin cups and bake at 400 degrees for 20–25 minutes.

Chocolate Chip Muffins (makes 12)

- 1¾ cups quick mix
- ¾ cup sugar
- ½ cup wheat flour
- ¼ cup rolled oats
- 1 tsp. vanilla
- 1 egg
- 1½ cups water
- 1 cup chocolate chips
- ½ cup chopped nuts (opt.)

Mix well. Spoon into sprayed muffin cups. Bake at 400 degrees for 20–25 minutes.

Chocolate Dessert Muffins (makes 12–14)

- 1¾ cups quick mix
- ¾ cup wheat flour
- 1 cup sugar
- 5 Tbsp. baking cocoa
- ½ cup chopped nuts (opt.)
- 1 cup chocolate chips
- ⅓ cup applesauce
- 1 egg
- 1½ cups water

Mix well. Spoon into sprayed muffin cups. Bake at 375 degrees for 20–23 minutes.

Coffee Cake Muffins (makes 12)

    1¾ cups quick mix
    ½ cup wheat flour
    ¼ cup sugar
    ¾ cup water

Mix just until moistened. Spoon half of the batter into sprayed muffin cups.

STREUSEL:

    ¼ cup brown sugar
    ¼ cup chopped nuts
    1 Tbsp. flour
    1 tsp. cinnamon
    1 Tbsp. melted butter

Spoon streusel onto batter. Spoon remaining batter on top of the streusel mixture. Bake at 350 degrees for 20 minutes. If last half of batter gets too thick while the topping is being made, add 1–2 tablespoon water and stir before placing the remainder on top of muffins.

Cornmeal Muffins (makes 12 muffins)

    1¾ cups quick mix
    2 Tbsp. sugar
    1 cup cornmeal
    1 tsp. baking powder
    1 egg
    1½ cups water.

Mix dry ingredients. Add egg and water; mix well. Spoon batter into sprayed muffin cups, or pour into a greased 8 x 8 baking dish. Bake at 400 degrees 20–25 minutes.

Maple Muffins (makes 12–15)

  1¾ cups quick mix
  1 cup rolled oats (quick or regular)
  ½ cup maple syrup
  ¼ cup applesauce
  ½ cup water

GLAZE:

  ½ cup powdered sugar
  2 Tbsp. maple syrup

Mix, then spoon into sprayed muffin cups. Bake at 400 degrees for 18–20 minutes. Remove from oven. While still hot, spread glaze over top of cooked muffins.

Oatmeal Muffins (makes 12)

  1¾ cups quick mix
  1 cup rolled oats (quick or regular)
  2 Tbsp. sugar
  1½ cups water

Mix gently until ingredients are moistened. Spoon batter into sprayed muffin cups and bake at 375 degrees for 20–25 minutes.

Peanut Butter Muffins (makes 18)

- 1¾ cups quick mix
- ¾ cup wheat flour
- ¼ cup sugar
- ½ cup peanut butter (creamy or chunky)
- 1 egg
- 1¼ cups water

Combine quick mix, wheat flour, and sugar. Cut in peanut butter until mixture is crumbly. Add egg and water. Mix well, then spoon into sprayed muffin cups. Place ½ teaspoon jelly in the middle of each muffin before baking. Bake at 400 degrees for 15–17 minutes.

Poppy Seed Muffins (makes 12)

- 1¾ cup quick mix
- 1 cup wheat flour
- ¼ tsp. nutmeg
- 5 tsp. poppy seeds
- ½ cup chopped pecans (opt.)
- 1¼ cups orange juice or water

Mix well. Spoon into sprayed muffin cups. Bake at 375 degrees for 20 minutes.

Pumpkin Muffins (makes 12–15)

  1¾ cups quick mix
  ½ cup wheat flour
  ½ tsp. cinnamon
  ¼ tsp. nutmeg
  2 Tbsp. sugar
  ½ cup water
  ½ cup mashed, cooked pumpkin
  ½ cup of chopped nuts or chocolate chips (opt.)

Mix gently, but well, and spoon into sprayed muffin cups. Bake at 400 degrees for 20 minutes.

Whole Wheat Breakfast Muffins (makes 12)

  1¾ cups quick mix
  ¾ cup whole wheat or white flour
  1½ cups water
  ½ cup chopped nuts (opt.)

Mix well. Spoon batter into sprayed muffin cups. Bake at 375 degrees for 20 minutes.

Pancakes and Waffles

Whole Wheat, Buttermilk Pancakes or Waffles

1¾ cups quick mix
¼ tsp. baking soda
1 egg
1¼ cups buttermilk

Mix well. Pour onto sprayed griddle or well sprayed waffle iron. Cook until done.

Whole Wheat, Pancakes

1¾ cups quick mix
1¼ cups water
1 egg

Stir well, then pour onto hot griddle. Cook over medium heat until tops are bubbly. Then flip pancakes and finish cooking. Serve with warm applesauce or maple syrup.

Blueberry Pancakes

Sprinkle 1–2 tablespoon blueberries on each pancake when you first place the batter on the griddle. Flip and bake other side.

Pecan Pancakes

Sprinkle ½ tablespoon chopped pecans on each pancake when you first place the batter on the griddle. Flip and bake other side.

Quick Breads and Cakes

Cranberry Nut Bread

1¾ cups quick mix
1 cup wheat flour
½ tsp. baking soda
¾ cup sugar
1 Tbsp. grated orange peel
1½ cups chopped cranberries
1 cup orange juice or water
½ cup chopped nuts (opt.)

Preheat oven to 350 degrees. Mix ingredients well and pour into greased 9 x 5 loaf pan. Bake for 55 minutes.

Lemon Bread

1¾ cups quick mix
¾ cup wheat flour
⅔ cup sugar
½ cup chopped nuts (opt.)
grated rind from 2 lemons
1 egg
¾ cup water

Preheat oven to 350 degrees. Combine quick mix, wheat flour, sugar, nuts, and grated lemon rind. Add egg and water. Mix well, then spoon into sprayed 9 x 5 loaf pan and bake 1 hour.

After removing from oven, pour 1 cup powdered sugar mixed with the juice of 2 lemons over top of loaf. Cool and slice.

Whole Wheat Carrot Cake

1¾ cup quick mix
1 cup wheat flour
½ tsp. baking soda
¼ tsp. salt
2 tsp. cinnamon
1¾ cups sugar
2 eggs
3 cups grated raw carrots
1 can of crushed pineapple (20 oz., with juice)
1 cup chopped pecans and/or raisins (opt.)

Preheat oven to 325 degrees. Mix dry ingredients well. Add eggs, carrots, pineapple, and nuts or raisins. Bake in greased, floured 9 x 13 pan for 1 hour and 10 minutes. Top with cream cheese frosting or orange glaze. Cut when cool

CREAM CHEESE FROSTING

4 cups powdered sugar
1 tsp. vanilla
3 oz. softened cream cheese
3 Tbsp. softened butter

Mix all ingredients well. Add enough milk or cream to make frosting a spreading consistency

ORANGE GLAZE

1 cup powdered sugar
1 tsp. vanilla
½ cup orange juice concentrate

Mix well and pour over warm cake.

Conclusion

Regardless of what type of mill you use or what type of bread mixer you have—or if you don't have one at all—you can incorporate whole grain or whole wheat bread into your diet. With good whole wheat flour and a willingness to try something new (or old), you can find good health and much satisfaction in learning the principles of good whole wheat bread making. Finally, you will undoubtedly create wonderful memories of home for those you love. I wish you success in your whole wheat bread making and baking endeavors.

Personal Notes and Recipes

Diana Ballard

Diana Ballard has been making whole wheat bread for 35 years. Because of the challenges of whole wheat bread making, she has spent many hours searching for answers to questions about the process. After thoroughly research-ing whole wheat bread making, Diana has written this book to share the secrets known by professional bakers, cereal chemists, and educators. Diana is married to Larry L. Ballard and lives in Salem, Utah. She and her husband are the parents of five children and twelve grandchildren, all of whom have many memories of hot wheat bread from Mama's kitchen.